EVERYTHING I LEARNED ABOUT SALES I LEARNED FROM MY DOG

BUTT SNIFFING IS NOT A VIRTUE

JULIE HICKEY, MBA

NIGHT
RIVER
PRESS

ISBN: 978-1-7347660-1-1 (Paperback).
ISBN: 978-1-7347660-0-4 (eBook).
Library of Congress Control Number: 2020908413

Any references to historical events, real people, or real places are used fictitiously. Names, characters, and places are products of the author's imagination.

Book cover and interior design by Susan Malikowski
Cover pup illustration by Rinartdy17
Book edited by Bess Maher and Victoria Walker
Cover photo by Nicole Wickens at www.greendoorphotography.com
Printed by Night River Press LLC, in the United States of America

First printing edition 2021.
Night River Press Denver, CO 80209
www.NightRiverPress.com

Contents

PREFACE vii

ONE ALWAYS HUNGRY 13
- Spoiler Alert! Quotas Always Go Up
- Make Sure You Are Getting Your Needs Met or Look for Something Else

TWO BUTT SNIFFING 23
- Listen First, Talk Later
- Take Time to Talk to Your Customers on a Personal Level

THREE DOGS NEED LOTS OF ATTENTION 27
- Build Customer Trust through Engagement
- Remember to Nurture Relationships

FOUR YOU ARE THE CENTER OF THEIR UNIVERSE . . 39
- Focus on Their Needs
- Build Long-Term Relationships by Being Attentive and Authentic, Even in Transactional Sales

FIVE GOTTA GO NOW! 47
- Customer Urgency
- Figure Out the Customer Timeline Up Front So There Are No Surprises

SIX OOPS! 55
- Mistakes Will Happen: Clean Them Up Quickly and Without Anger
- How You Handle Mistakes Is More Important Than the Mistake Itself

SEVEN A CHOW CHOW IS NOT A LAB
IS NOT A BEAGLE 59
- Let Them Tell You What's Important
  to Them Before Diving into Your
  Sales Pitch

EIGHT FETCH (AGAIN AND AGAIN) 67
- Continuous Customer Contact Is Key
- Continue to Market to the Same Group

NINE ROLL DOWN THE WINDOW AND TAKE
IN THE SMELLS 75
- If You're Passionate about Your Product
  or Service, It Will Show
- Notice Customer Signals Along the Way
  and Be Prepared to Go Off Track

TEN I'M NOT GOING IN THERE: THE VET 83
- Checkups and Check-Ins Are Important
  to Any Relationship
- Use Dashboards to Measure Your
  Progress and See Where You Need
  to Put More Attention

ELEVEN DOG PARK RULES 91
- How to Work with Complex
  Organizations
- How to Navigate Various Personalities

TWELVE BAD DOG. 97
- How to Handle Bad Customers
- What to Do If You Have a Bad Boss

THIRTEEN STAY HYDRATED 103
- Focus on Work/Life Balance
- Take Care of Yourself or You'll Never
  Survive Long Term in Sales

FOURTEEN SHAKE OFF THE MUD 111
- Change Your Mindset
- Be Prepared to Zig Instead of Zag

FIFTEEN SOMETIMES THEIR BARK IS WORSE
THAN THEIR BITE 119
- Dealing with Angry Customers
- It's Not You

SIXTEEN BE TRUE TO YOURSELF: DON'T TRY
TO BE A PITBULL IF YOU ARE A POODLE 127
- How to Navigate the Old Boys
  Network If You Aren't Part of It

SEVENTEEN DON'T FORGET TO ROLL AROUND IN THE
MUD, GET DIRTY, AND HAVE SOME FUN 133
- Work Hard but Don't Forget to Stop
  and Laugh
- It's OK to Share Customer Stories,
  but Be Appropriate and Never Mean

ABOUT THE AUTHOR 137

Preface

I have been in sales for over thirty years and have learned a lot, or so I thought. Oddly enough, it was hanging out at our local dog park that educated me in a way my MBA never did. Over a year ago, when our golden Lab named Noe was old and in pain, we thought she needed a playmate. In hindsight, we waited too long and Noe completely ignored, and even considered a nuisance, our new golden retriever puppy, Oliver. As Oliver was bursting with puppy energy, I started taking him to the dog park before or after work.

We had recently moved into a neighborhood that had a nearby dog park, so I could easily walk there or drive when I was short on time or feeling lazy. I started to notice patterns in the dogs and how they related to each other. I watched how they all crowded at the entrance to greet the new dogs and sniff their butts to say hello. Some dogs were submissive; some were dominant. I noticed that Oliver played rough with certain dogs but gently with others. I saw the various ways the dogs interacted with each other, and I realized there were similarities to what I experienced in my sales job every day.

It made me reflect on my career as a salesperson and the patterns I've noticed with customer behavior and the ways I interact with my customers. There were so many similarities between the dog park dynamics and my experiences in the sales arena that I decided to put them on paper. As you can see from the names of the chapters, the overlap is as profound as it is comical. I subscribe to the philosophy that you should not take yourself too seriously. If you enjoy my insights, feel free to laugh out loud, especially if you are in church or on an airplane.

Here's a little about me so you'll get a feeling for who I am. I am a mom, wife, daughter, sister, friend, dog owner, career salesperson, book lover, traveler, entrepreneur, parenting blogger on the www.theordinarymom.com, side hustle blogger on www.thesidehustlejourney.com, and now a published author. I don't pretend to know everything about sales or life, but I learn new things every day and hope to be a lifelong learner. In this book, I share some of my thoughts and experiences that I hope will help you on your sales journey. Or if you picked this book up by mistake because you saw the cute dog on the cover (that's our Oliver), I hope it entertains you and you learn at least one new thing.

Here are my core beliefs about sales. They are at the heart of this book. Be real, be honest (most of the time), and put yourself in your customers' shoes and figure out how you can make their lives easier. Even though we all need to make money, don't do it just for money. Find something else that makes your job, and future sales jobs, fulfilling because if you're miserable, you will make everyone around you miserable. No one will want to buy from you, or in dog speak, no one will want to sniff your butt.

If you're already in sales, some of what I advise will be the same things that you do day in and day out. But I hope this take will give you a more comedic and creative lens to view your career challenges. Who knows? Our four-legged friends may be the best life coaches out there. And if you take away one or two nuggets from this book and apply them to your work, then I did my job.

A career in sales is not always easy. It's filled with ups and downs and can be very stressful, especially when you're striving for the ever-growing quota. Just remember that prospects and customers are a lot like dogs: They need a lot of attention, they like to be scratched behind their ears, and sometimes they "gotta go now." (I'm assuming you know I'm using metaphors and you won't really scratch your clients behind their ears. That could get really awkward, and no one wants HR involved.) If you find the humor in a difficult situation, you can get through it more easily.

One note about the dog metaphors in this book: Sometimes you are the dog, always hungry for more sales. Sometimes your customers, or even your colleagues, are the dog and you are the long-suffering and ever-patient owner. I've used the dog metaphor in whatever way it makes sense to help us navigate this rewarding but sometimes stressful career.

I am so grateful to have worked with so many amazing

sales folks in my career. There are too many to mention, but I do want to thank those who have taught me to stay true to myself, to work hard even when I don't feel like it, to pick myself up when I get knocked down, and, most importantly, to laugh a lot. Thanks to the following sales folks who have made an indelible difference in my life listed in order of when we worked together: Lindsay, Paige, Rene, Marcy, Holly, MK, CD, Ralph, Gordon, Sharon, Marie, Mike C., Marisa, Kevin, Page P., and Gary.

I also want to thank my wife and kids for supporting me in this career choice that is often unpredictable in both pay and work hours. I'm glad that they still love me even when I come home from a long day and I'm tired and grumpy. (This happens more than I'd like to admit.) I want to thank my sister, Lisa, for supporting me to be a writer like she is and for offering her suggestions and edits on this book; my brother, Mike, a fellow salesperson; and my Aunt Robin, an accomplished businessperson, for both reviewing an early copy of the book and for offering edits and smart suggestions. I'd also like to thank my dad for being the most amazing salesperson I've ever met and for giving me sage career advice throughout my life. Finally, I want to express my appreciation to my mom for always believing in me and teaching me to "keep on keeping on."

I want to thank my copy editors, Bess Maher and Victoria Walker, my book cover and interior designer, Susan Malikowski, and my amazing long-time friend, mentor, and editor, Skeeter Buck of Night River Press.

I have made some new friends at the dog park who have made my life better because they are in it. You know who you are, so thank you, Dog Park Goddesses.

Last but certainly not least, I want to thank my dogs, and all dogs, for showing me what my bosses, colleagues, and business professors never could teach me about the nature of people and sales.

CHAPTER ONE

Always Hungry

SPOILER ALERT! QUOTAS ALWAYS GO UP

Just like dogs, sales managers are always hungry. I'm going to say something revolutionary here. . . . Quotas always go up. If you haven't figured that out by now, either you are not in sales or you have been surprised and frustrated year after year that no matter how good you are, your quota is always higher the next year. If you hit your quota one year, management tends to increase your quota by at least 10 to 15 percent the next year. (It may go up even more if you are in a fast-growing industry or at a start-up.)

As a career salesperson, I have never been a big fan of this top-down way of forecasting. I think realistic forecasting should be bottom-up rather than top-down. Top-down forecasting is when your company has set expectations, e.g., a 20 percent growth rate year after year, and they push down those expectations to the different business units to achieve or beat that goal. For public companies, if they have publicly stated they will grow 15 percent in the next year, they may push that number down the chain to achieve that goal. It doesn't have to be the same for every business line or product, but they need to set expectations and quotas that average at least a 15 percent annual growth.

To do bottom-up forecasting, you look at what you have in the pipeline and factor in any changes, e.g., new products, more marketing, and extra resources to assist the salespeople, and then come up with a realistic goal. You may need to spread out expectations across the organization where some high-growth areas are expected to grow more than an older, established product line that is not releasing any new products. You still need to achieve your goals, but you do it in a realistic way based on what new products and opportunities are in the pipeline and not just, "You need to achieve a 20 percent growth even though we have no new products or no potential sales." I'm all for having a goal you have to stretch for, but it should be realistic and attainable based on the sales territory.

Once I had a 25 percent year-over-year quota increase with no new products or services coming out in the next year, no extra marketing scheduled, and no large potential sales in the pipeline. When I looked at the last five years of my territory, I noticed that when you took the five-year average and increased it by 10 percent, it became my new 25 percent quota. I pointed out to my management that one of those years was the best sales year ever for the territory because we had just released a revolutionary new product. I suggested that we throw out that one crazy high year as an outlier and then average the remaining years and apply the 10 percent growth. The finance team did not agree to that, so I started the year knowing that I was set up for failure. I ended up moving into a new role in the same company midway through the year because I was given an impossible goal with no extra support or new products to help me reach the goal.

I am on a sales team now that appreciates having seasoned salespeople. My management team (who were all salespeople promoted from within the company, yay!) realizes that if they make quotas unrealistic or unattainable for a particular territory, they will have salesforce turnover. Then they have to spend more time and money finding a new person to hire and bring up to speed.

MAKE SURE YOU ARE GETTING YOUR NEEDS MET OR LOOK FOR SOMETHING ELSE

Just as sales managers can be hungrier than a growing puppy, sales professionals also have needs that must be met. Good managers realize that veteran salespeople are not a dime a dozen. There is a huge value in keeping salespeople happy so they don't company hop. If you are reading this and are in management, just remember that salespeople get requests from recruiters all the time. Every time we don't take a new job, we've made a choice to stay where we are because we are happy and/or we see potential.

For the sales folks reading this, make sure you are

getting what you need from your company to be happy. And remember: happiness doesn't come just from money. Make sure you feel the company is providing you with quality products and appropriate compensation such as salary, commission, bonuses, stock, good health insurance, life insurance, vision insurance, and maybe extras like a company car (or at least pay for gas and car usage), phone, computer, tablet, marketing support, and technical support. Make sure your company provides a culture that fits with your values and your lifestyle. If you do not feel valued at your current company, make a long-term plan and work backwards to meet that goal.

My dad always said it's easier to find a job when you have a job. This is so true. In my experience, the easiest way to find a job is when you are happy in your current job and not even looking. If you're happy in your current position and you pass on a job opportunity, do so in a way that keeps the door open in case your situation changes. If you find yourself unhappy at your current job with no other prospects, try to fake it until you find a new job. Pull from that reservoir of strength I know is in you. (You are a salesperson, after all, so I know you're strong!) Grit your teeth, put on a fake smile if you have to, make a plan to get a new job, and go get it. Don't look back.

If you're doing well at your current job and a recruiter contacts you, let that happiness and confidence shine through. I am lucky to be in the position that I am content in my current role at my company of seven years. In the last few years when a recruiter has asked if I'm interested in a different role, I've honestly said, "I like my current company and am knocking it out of the ballpark this year. But if you brought me the perfect job, of course I would consider it." Recruiters have stopped bringing me lateral moves. It saves both the recruiters and me time and energy, knowing I'm only willing to listen to job opportunities that will catapult me into a new sphere.

A company's culture plays a big role in whether you're happy there. For instance, a company that values its employees and supports work/life balance is very important to me. As a working parent, I'm cautious when a recruiter brings me a position from a start-up. I worked at several start-ups when I was younger and have found that the pay wasn't that great and they overwork their employees based on the premise that everyone is going to make it big.

Start-up culture can be great, but it's not for everyone. I find that start-ups tend to be unrealistic about what you can make as a salesperson. Being a new company, there tends to be more optimism than data. They tend to say, "You have the ability to make $X—a huge number like a million dollars—a year." The problem is almost no one ever makes a million dollars in sales a year at a start-up.

"What did the salespeople make last year?" I always ask the recruiter. I usually get something like, "Well, they made a lot less but that was the first year and now the company is more established and the product is selling like gangbusters." Or they may point to that one salesperson who made a million dollars. In that case, I would ask if they can put something in writing guaranteeing a minimum amount that would make the jump to a start-up worth it for you. Don't be surprised if they don't (they never have for me).

I also see red flags when they talk about the five cafeterias with all different kinds of food their world-renowned chefs will prepare. (This means you will be working around the clock and eating all of your meals at work!)

I see a really big red flag when I'm told it's a start-up and they are not offering any equity for the stress of riding on the roller coaster with them, which means that they aren't willing to do what it takes to attract high level employees. And if they do make it big, which is unlikely, the employees won't get to share in the profits. I bow out quickly and politely and move on. At this point in my career, I'm not willing to move to a start-up that doesn't want to compensate me in both pay and stock to make up for the risk of leaving a good job at a stable company. I don't feel it's my job to take all of the risks of a new company but not get any of the rewards. For now, I'll stick to my big, established company with strong brands, good benefits, and consistent pay. If you are young and not supporting a family and see real potential in the company, go for it. For those of us who have been around a while, we have watched so many start-ups begin with optimism and passion but then fizzle out and die in a few years.

As a reminder, never talk negatively about your current company to a recruiter. We are only as good as our current job and that job could be taken from us tomorrow.

Things look a lot different when you are unemployed. Remember, if you get laid off, you're going to be the one who needs to contact recruiters, ASAP. I'm a believer that you should throw things out to the universe and see what comes back. That's why you should turn down job offers in a way that leaves the door open, or, depending on your situation, establishes expectations. I also keep a list of recruiters and am generous about sending that list to friends who have been laid off. One friend got a job within two weeks of being laid off and credits a lot of the speed to my list of recruiters. Always bring people up when they are down because it's the right thing to do, and people will remember if you helped them when they needed it.

Recently, a recruiter was telling me about a role that was a lateral move at a company not as well known as my current company. I wanted to stay on his list for future roles, so I decided to take a very honest approach that he would either appreciate or not. (If he did, he'd only bring me the cream of the crop of future job openings.) I am copying the wording I sent to him for your reference:

> *To be totally transparent, I have found that every time I've talked to a recruiter in the last few years, the prospective company can't come anywhere near my current compensation, so I have had no motivation to change companies (fyi, I made $X last year and, in full disclosure, it was a good year). I have been doing high tech/educational sales for almost thirty years and am happy at ABC company; however, I'd never turn down*

my dream job. Here is my dream job: in a field that I love (i.e., education, writing, travel, or something that allows me to be an entrepreneur), doing meaningful work, mostly home based without too much travel (I'm tired from traveling for so many years), making a guaranteed $X/year for a company that values its employees above all else with an amazing culture and truly supports work/life balance.

The funny thing is, after sending this email to the recruiter the conversation switched from trying to place me in that lateral job to trying to hire me for the recruiting company. It turns out it wasn't my ideal job, so I'm still happily at the same company, but he has me on his radar if he ever comes across anything that seems like my ideal job.

Once again, think about those dogs at the dog park. You can never throw down a treat without them going for it. They stay hungry, or in our case, open to a better position. They also know what they want, and they go for it. Decide what your perfect role looks like, write it down, and then put it out there. You can't expect people to read your mind. It's like expecting your dog to retrieve the ball before you've thrown it. It's unrealistic and won't happen. Know what you want and don't settle for less.

Sometimes, you are in a situation where you have to get a job ASAP. That's OK. It happens. Just secure employment and then make a longer-term plan to achieve something better. One of my dog park friends got laid off from a secure, well-known company in Silicon Valley. He ended up taking another job with a terrible commute. He knew he couldn't do it forever, but he took the job knowing he could do it for a year. In the meantime, while he was employed, he worked on finding a better job closer to home. We all have to make short-term sacrifices to get to our bigger goal. You'll get there. Just stay hungry. Remember what you want.

CHAPTER TWO

Butt Sniffing

LISTEN FIRST, TALK LATER

A nyone with dogs knows that when dogs first meet, they often sniff each other's butt. To humans, this seems like an odd and unsanitary thing to do, but to dogs, it's like reading people's online profile before you meet them—you find out about their history and get a sense of who they are. Dogs have an incredible sense of smell, so by butt sniffing, they can find out whether or not the other dog is aggressive, sick, friendly, and so forth. Other than the butt-sniffing part, we should all borrow a page from our dog's book: taking the time to assess your clients is invaluable.

As a salesperson, you can size up your customers in a few ways. If you are meeting in person, notice the person's stance or body language when you first meet. Is there a genuine smile on his face that shows warmth and receptiveness, or is he guarded? Does she take the time to ask how you are doing today, or does she jump right into business? You can get a good sense of someone's personality and demeanor if you take the time to observe their signals and body language. But again, please don't sniff their butt!

After sizing them up, take a bit more time to get to know them better. It will help you understand them and be a better salesperson for them. For instance, I was at a meeting recently and talked to my customer during a break. He had been "that customer" with a lot of special requests, making things harder than they needed to be. On the break, I told him how my three kids were at three different schools this year and how challenging it was. I mentioned that we had moved the youngest from a public to a private school. He asked why, and I answered that she was recently diagnosed with dyslexia and had a lot of anxiety and social issues last year and we felt we needed to change her environment. He opened up that he grew up with dyslexia but didn't get diagnosed until after college. He said it has always been difficult for him to read for fun.

We then discussed how becoming a social studies teacher was an interesting choice—lots of reading for that—and we talked about how he works hard every day to overcome his reading challenges. Once I heard his story, I felt more empathetic towards him for the rest of the meeting. I realized that he had his own struggles to overcome and those struggles might even have been why I had labeled him as challenging. Connecting with my customer allowed me to be more understanding and to see things from his point of view. It allowed me to be a better salesperson for him.

If you are dealing with customers on the phone or via email, it's much harder to get to know them and develop a rapport. Phone calls are usually more business focused with less time to get a sense of one another or break the ice. However, it's still important to take time to get to know the customer on a personal level. This may not happen on the first phone call, so don't feel the need to hound your customer with questions at first. That said, make sure that you are actively listening and if your customer mentions anything personal, then follow up on it. If you can move a sale from being transactional to relationship-based, it will make your customers feel more invested in you and the relationship. Next time they want to buy something, they will remember the value you brought to the table. Everyone wants to be heard and treated with respect, so try to be the salesperson who does that with your customers.

TAKE TIME TO TALK TO YOUR CUSTOMERS ON A PERSONAL LEVEL

Sometimes we don't always take the time to connect with customers when we should. When I was in sales in Silicon Valley, I attended a quarterly business review with an important client, a big computer manufacturer that sold our software. We had brought in the Big Dog, the Senior Vice President (SVP) of Sales. She is unbelievably smart and taught me so much in the fifteen years I worked with her. She can read any situation quickly and adjust accordingly. I'm grateful to her for the mentorship and, later, friendship. That day when we did introductions, the customer's VP said his grandmother had just died and he was feeling down. My SVP responded with something like, "Sorry about your grandmother, but let's get down to business." It was extremely brusque, and she didn't show much sympathy, nor did she ask any follow-up questions about his grandmother.

In hindsight, she realized what she had done and felt terrible about it. The meeting went fine, but she and I still laugh about that gaffe—not about the fact that his grandmother died (which I'm sure was horrible) but about the way she bulldozed past his vulnerability and pain and moved directly onto business. She told me later that she kept in touch with that customer and that they eventually became friends, so I don't think he held it against her or maybe he didn't even realize how brusque she had been. Still, keep this story in mind if someone opens up and shows their vulnerability or tells you something painful or personal in a meeting or in a side conversation. Take a moment to acknowledge it and ask a heartfelt follow-up question so your prospect can feel heard.

We're all animals, so follow the example of those dogs at the dog park and take the time to watch your customers' body language and try to get to know who they are and what they need in the moment and in a product or service. Remember, there is a purpose to sniffing butts, and dogs, just like humans, are better off knowing as much as possible about their fellow canines from the very beginning.

CHAPTER THREE

Dogs Need Lots of Attention

BUILD CUSTOMER TRUST THROUGH ENGAGEMENT

Sales is not always about sales: it's also about building customer trust that will get you closer to an actual sale. With dogs, you build their trust by being consistent in your love, attention, discipline, feeding, walking, and so forth. Just like dogs, prospects and customers need lots of attention in order to build trust. Consistent customer engagement develops trust and leads to healthy, long-term relationships.

Sometimes I'm not able to provide the consistent attention my dog needs. I remember a particularly busy time last year when I was traveling every day for two weeks for work. My family was able to feed and walk our dog in my absence, but he didn't get the extra walks or time at that dog park that he's used to. Because of that, Oliver dug up the newly planted lemon tree in the back-yard that my wife and I had so carefully picked out and planted. This is similar to what can happen if you don't give your customers enough attention. They may not eat your lemon tree, but they may lash out in other ways.

I try to remember that so much of my life happens outside of my house, but dogs spend most of their time at the house and we are the most important thing in their lives. Every morning when I get up, I get on the ground, scratch my dog, call him "good boy," and spend a few minutes enjoying this simple pleasure and connection. And even though I'm usually in a hurry when I come into the house, I remember that my dog has been waiting to see his humans and that we are the center of his universe. I build his trust by taking care of him, taking him to the dog park, and taking the extra time to get down to his level and scratch him behind the ears and rub his belly. It also calms me, makes me stop and take a moment to do what is important, nurtures a relationship that makes us both happy, and gives me joy.

For my prospects and customers, I can't honestly say they all bring me joy. (Sorry, Marie Kondo, but I can't throw them out.) However, I want to do right by them, build trust, and nurture those relationships in a real and meaningful way. Most of your prospects and customers deal with a lot of vendors and can see through those who are not authentic and are only interested in hitting their quotas. It's important to be attentive to them consistently. Remember that someday you may need them more than they need you, so when they need your attention and help, do your best to give it them. You can guarantee that they will remember what you did when they needed you.

For example, in the educational publishing business

where I work now, there is a cycle for how school districts adopt products. For the most part, customers evaluate products in the fall, pilot ("test drive") two or three products in the winter and early spring, decide what to buy in mid- to late spring, order in June or July, and implement in late summer to prepare for back to school. It's an annual cycle rarely deviated from unless there's extra money at another time of year through grants or the customer gets back to school and realizes they have new classes or need more curriculum.

So from the salesperson standpoint, we work really hard trying to sell from fall to early summer. But from the customer standpoint, their most important time is mid-July to late September when they are getting the products up and running when the students get back to school. Even though I'm doing the least amount of selling in the six to eight weeks of late summer and early fall, it is the busiest—and the most stressful—time of the year for me. This is the time when my customers are trying to implement what they have purchased from me and will either look at the purchase as being a success or a failure. Even though I work for a big company, their memory of whether the product was successful usually falls on me and how much I helped them when they needed it. I'm not selling as much during this back-to-school time, but I understand the importance of making sure that my customers get what they need when they need it most and that they are up and running successfully during this time.

Tensions are high at this time, and my customers have

a "gotta have it now" focus. For me, this time is filled with lots of administrative work, shipment tracking, and tech support issues. I often get the same questions or complaints over and over. I prioritize what they need and try to be extremely responsive so that they know that they can count on me when they need me, not just when I need something from them, i.e., an order. I have found that by working my hardest and trying to prioritize which customers really do "gotta have it now," my customers remember my efforts when they are looking at which publishers to buy other products from.

Prioritizing can be difficult. My biggest customers get my attention first, and though I try not to forget the smaller ones, sometimes they may have to wait. The irony is that in education, like in many industries, I have found the smaller the school district, the more they expect a fast turnaround. Sometimes the smaller ones are the ones who yell the loudest and then you get off track by attending to their needs. They also tend to be the ones that escalate to my management during this time of year if they feel they aren't getting what they need. This is often true, so I just try to give my boss a heads-up that she may get a call from someone complaining about me.

I also have some things that I can do during this crazy time to appease customers, like ship a small free product or expedite the customer's shipping. I use these perks sparingly and usually only do it when my company has made a mistake or shipped the wrong thing. It can often be the make-good I need to save a relationship when my company didn't live up to the customer's expectations.

Sometimes I use these perks to help my bigger customers in order to maintain a strong relationship with
them. Recently, my contact at an important district who
has always been good to me said, "I forgot to order X for
back to school and now I am going to get in big trouble
from my boss." In this instance, I decided to help her. I
told her to send the order directly to me instead of the
usual process of going through customer service so that I
could push it through. I also expedited the shipping at no
charge that one time. The customer was so grateful because I helped her when she needed it and she was able
to save face with her boss. She will certainly remember
that I went above and beyond for her. I did it because
she's always been good to me and I wanted to reciprocate
that in our relationship.

Another way that I try to build customer trust is by
being honest with them when I make a mistake. I'm
always juggling what seems like one hundred things at
once, and sometimes I forget to do something or don't
follow through on a promise I made. I have found that
many salespeople lie or blame someone else when they
get called out, but I always try to be honest and say, "I'm
so sorry, I forgot to do that," or, "You are correct that you
had emailed me that on that date, but I must have missed
it in my email."

As much as it's hard to take the blame and have your
customers be upset at you, it's the right thing to do. In
the long run, my customers usually appreciate that I was
honest and took responsibilty for my actions. This approach is doubly true in big companies. I could easily say

things like, "The order got stuck in our system," "The warehouse must be really backed up," or "Customer service lost that order." I try to be above those excuses because I understand how important trust is in any long-term relationship. In full disclosure, I have passed blame to customer service, our warehouse, or third-party shipping companies when it was my fault on occasions when the customer was exceedingly angry. I thought I needed to stay out of the crosshairs because admitting to a mistake to that particular customer at that particular time would damage our long-term relationship.

Sometimes it's possible to take the blame in a tense situation without damaging the relationship. I'll never forget a time when I was working in Silicon Valley and we had to meet with a big computer manufacturer to tell them we changed our product and now they would be required to pay for something that had been free to them. The meeting went terribly (as expected). Fortunately, my boss went with me to take responsibility for the changes so that I could maintain a positive relationship with this important customer. Our contact at the company was this (usually) lovely French guy who had been a really good customer to us. However, on that day, he was so mad he cut the meeting short and escorted us out.

As we were almost to the exit, my boss turned to him and said, "It's great to know that you live so close to me. Would you and your wife like to get together with me and my wife soon for dinner?" Our customer was clearly disarmed by this comment after our disastrous meeting, but he said, "Sure, that sounds good." After we left the meeting, I was shocked and asked my boss how he had the nerve to say that to our customer as we were being kicked out of the meeting. His response was something like, "Just because he didn't like what we were saying in the meeting doesn't mean that we have to throw the whole relationship out the window." It was a gutsy move, but my boss genuinely liked the customer, wanted to get to know him better, and was sincere that he wanted to befriend him outside the workplace. It must have worked because we were able to get the relationship back on track and all was well from that point forward.

Trust is not just about the big things. Trust can be built up over time with lots of little things. For instance, I never promise I can do something today or commit to offering a discount or free product when I know I can't. You will actually make the customer happier if you say, "I know this is important to you and I will get it done as soon as possible, but I have to rely on other folks to get some of this information, so it may take me a few days to get back to you with an answer." In this way, you are building trust while setting honest and realistic deadlines or expectations.

REMEMBER TO NURTURE RELATIONSHIPS

Nurturing business relationships is just as important as nurturing personal relationships. But the key word is "nurture." It takes time. When I start a new position or take on new customers, I don't pretend like I know everything about them or their company and that we are best friends. The reality is that it is a business relationship and we are not friends, and honestly, we probably won't ever become friends. I find people who act this way to be disingenuous and have seen it with salespeople at every company I've worked for.

It's unrealistic to think—or pretend—that you're best friends with someone whom you just met. (I can think of only a few times in my life that I became real friends with someone right away and never in a business setting.) This is work, so the goal is not to try to be best friends with your prospects or customers but to have a good working relationships with them. In the thirty years I've been in sales, I have several customers I stay in touch with, but the only real friends I've made at work were colleagues. Maybe I am too rigid or professional with my customers, but I have seen too many people I work with try to befriend their customers in order to be successful in their jobs and it strikes me as forced and, sometimes, unprofessional. If you do end up being friends with your customers, that's an added bonus but not typical.

Even though you may never be real friends with your customers, you still need to nurture those relationships. Think of it in terms of having a dog and how you nurture that relationship, especially in the beginning. You need to provide them with the basics for their survival like food, water, sun, bathroom breaks, etc. But it's the extra attention like walks, dog park time, scratching behind their ears, rubbing their bellies, and just loving them that makes the relationship thrive. Same with customer relationships, although please don't scratch them behind their ears or give them a belly rub. That would be very awkward.

The basic things you need to do to maintain a relationship with your customers include answering their calls and emails, getting them information in a timely manner, and placing their orders. But it's the extra things like taking the time to know what problems they're trying to solve, finding out what would make their lives easier, calculating what they can afford to spend, or knowing when something is time sensitive to them and putting in extra work to hit their deadlines that go a long way. And if you can, figure out if they have personal things going on and remember to mention them (e.g., marriage, new baby, or illness).

I try to remember that my customers are human and they have things going on outside of work. As a working parent of three young kids, I certainly have things going on outside of work. Although I try not to spend too much time talking about my personal life to customers, I might mention an upcoming event or brag a little about my children to an associate. I appreciate when someone remembers and follows up on it. Most customer conversations will be about work-related things, but it's good to have a deeper relationship with your customers, when appropriate, and everyone appreciates it if you remember to mention something personal that they told you in the past, like a new baby or grandchild.

Just like dogs love a good scratch on their belly and behind their ears, your prospects and customers want attention, too. They might want to tell you what is going on in their lives but then forget to ask you what's going on in yours. They realize, either subconsciously or not, that they have an attentive audience who wants them to be happy because happy people are more likely to buy your product. There is a power play here because you usually need them more than they need you, which means you often have to defer to them. I know that is unfair but that's part of being in sales. You can have your pride or you can have your sale. Sadly, I'm only half joking about that.

In my experience, most prospects and customers do not take advantage of the power they have over me in my sales role, but occasionally I do find people take advantage of the fact that I need them more than they need me. We'll go into more detail in chapter 12, 'Bad Dog,' when it's OK to "bite back" when you feel you're being taken advantage of, but for this chapter, we'll assume that everyone is playing nice and no one is stealing food from your dog bowl.

To be clear, never be inauthentic or praise your customer when you don't mean it. Salespeople who are fake, lie, or just tell the prospect or customer what they want to hear bring a bad name to the profession. I believe the mission of this profession is to try to fill a need someone has with a product or service that will make their lives better or easier. If you're coming from that place, then the positive attention you give them will be authentic. If you can solve a customer's or prospect's need or pain point, do it in an authentic way, and charge them an amount that they will pay happily, or at least willingly, then you have done your job successfully.

At a dog park, the most beloved person is the one generously handing out treats or giving the dogs extra attention. They'll have the most dog friends by the end of the day, and they'll be remembered by those canines at subsequent visits. Be that person with your clients: always be ready to give them something extra, something kind, or something generous. If you can do that on top of giving your customers consistent attention, you will see a noticeable difference in your relationships with them.

CHAPTER FOUR

You Are the Center of Their Universe

FOCUS ON THEIR NEEDS

R emember that in sales, it's not about you, it's about them: the customers. Many salespeople make the mistake of thinking only about themselves: How am I going to hit my quota? What product can I make the most commission on? But what you really need to do is think about your customer's needs: What problem are they trying to solve? How can I become a trusted advisor to my customer? What can I offer them to make their lives easier? I'm not only talking about showering them with attention as discussed in the last chapter. I'm talking about looking at things from your customer's point of view, figuring out what they need, and acting accordingly.

In order to build healthy, long-term relationships, you need to focus on your client's needs in an authentic way. It's like when I get down on the floor to play with my dog. Even though I may feel like I have a hundred other things to do when I walk in my door, it's important to remember that we are the center of our pet's universe and they just want a little attention. Our dogs need a few dedicated moments when we pay attention to them, rub their bellies, and love them.

Even though I know I am not the center of the universe to my prospects and customers, they want to be the center of mine. Have you ever had a customer call you and say something like, "I emailed you an hour ago, and I still haven't heard back from you." Sometimes I want to tell them that I have fifty other customers that need my help or that I was sitting around all day waiting for their email and had just stepped away from my desk. Of course I don't say those things. Again, think of those little puppy eyes, staring at you when you come home from work. All they want is you—it's not selfish; it's just their nature. Like our dogs, our customers need to know that we make them our top priority at some point during our workday.

When I was a kid, I thought my stay-at-home mom was just sitting around waiting for all five of us to get home from school. I was clueless and didn't realize she was cleaning the house, doing the laundry for seven people, going grocery shopping, cooking food, running errands, and shuttling us to our activities and doctor's appointments. She was also doing everything for my dad so that he was able to work outside the home without any household obligations.

My mom never complained about her around-the-clock workload. In fact, that is the reason I was so clueless: she never talked about her other obligations. When she was with me, she always asked about my activities and my needs. Your clients should also be clueless about your other responsibilities. They should never know about your quotas or stresses. Give them the gift of cluelessness.

The exception is if you have a great relationship with a customer who would want to know if you hit your quota. I ended up hitting my quota this year—yay!—and I told one of my favorite customers that her order put me over my quota. (I told her after I had received her PO so I didn't influence her to order.) She was so happy to hear that I hit my quota and that her order helped. She was the only customer I mentioned my quota to all year as I am very selective about doing that. In fact, I can't think of another time in recent memory that I mentioned whether I was going to hit my quota to a customer because I try to focus on my customers' needs when I talk to them and not mine.

As hard as it is, if you can change to a mindset of thinking about what your customers' needs are instead of what yours are, you will see a notable difference in your business relationships. This does not mean I'm being naive about the quota you have to hit, the bills you have to pay, or the kids you need to get to doctor's appointments or soccer practices, but once you start thinking about how you can help your customers in an authentic way with the great product offering you have, you will become a much better salesperson. I discuss more ways to zero in on your customers' needs in chapter 7.

Also remember that most people work for other people and have a boss to worry about. My dad always told me the most important people in the company to keep happy are your boss and your boss's boss. Your customers will be grateful if you realize this truism applies to them as well. When they become needy, it's usually because their boss is pressuring them. Sometimes doing something as simple as noticing your client is stressed makes a big difference. If I can hear the stress in someone's voice or see it in their face, I always try to help.

Think of my example of the customer who meant to place an order and forgot because they were too busy. I realized I could help them get the order faster and save face with their boss if they sent the order directly to me. I then pushed it through the ordering process to get it done sooner. The customer was very grateful, and I'm sure they will remember that I went above and beyond to help them. Plus, I felt great because I like helping others.

BUILD LONG-TERM RELATIONSHIPS BY BEING ATTENTIVE AND AUTHENTIC, EVEN IN TRANSACTIONAL SALES

All of this directed attention on your customers and their needs is part of building long-term relationships with them. In some sales roles, though, it is not possible. You may be in a transactional selling business and only deal with the customer one time, in which case building long-term customer relationships is just not possible. I had that experience in my first real job when I sold computers at a large direct-to-consumer manufacturer. My first role was to answer incoming calls and sell them peripheral parts, e.g., printers, ink, or more memory. The customers had already purchased the computer with a more senior salesperson. Each call was an individual transaction, and they didn't have a way to get back in touch with me.

If they had more questions or wanted to buy something else, their call went back into the queue to the next available rep. In this situation, I was not able to develop long-term relationships with my customers; however, if I created a positive experience for them, they might call back or refer their friends and family to my company. Even though that might not benefit me directly, keeping customers coming back to order from the company that employs me is wise. In this case, think of yourself as the human at the dog park that all the dogs love.

One company that does transactional sales but is totally focused on customer service is United Services Automobile Association (USAA). USAA is my insurance company and you have to have a military affiliation to be a member. Lucky for me, my dad was in the military in his younger years when he was a handsome devil traveling the world as a naval officer. Insurance is not something I often think about. It's just something you have to pay for in life and hope you don't use very often.

USAA has created a company that is 100 percent customer focused and treats its customers with absolute respect. If you have a break-in or fender bender, the first thing USAA asks you is if you're okay. That may not seem like an important question, or may even sound a bit cliché, but their employees seem sincere. Next, they make it easy for you to get through what would normally be a terrible situation. If you had a car wreck, it gets you a rental car, tell you which body shop to go to, etc. Every time I get off the phone with USAA, I feel better than I did before I called. And we're talking about insurance! Imagine if all companies applied this same "customer first" mindset.

How is it that I can be happy when I get off the phone with my insurance company but feel like I want to hit something when I get off the phone with my cable company? I'm dependent on their products since I can't function without internet access and I look forward to watching my recorded and streaming shows in my downtime. It's just so painful to talk to the cable company that I dread it. Ironically, I'm happy with the product but not as a customer. Your number one rule of business should be to keep happy customers happy. If another company stepped in to provide decent internet and cable service and offered amazing customer service, I would bolt in a heartbeat. Keeping a happy customer happy is so much easier and less expensive than having to find and earn a new customer.

Similarly, I have an account I just could not crack. My contacts there were nice enough, but I could never make it a relationship sale—they wanted it to be more transactional. Over the last three years, I've been going in there as much as possible to develop relationships and, hopefully, to win some business. I had a breakthrough a few weeks ago when I sent an email to my favorite contact there to say I was going to be there the next day around noon and ask if she wanted to have lunch with me. I assumed she would say no, but she said yes. We went to lunch and had a great lunch mostly talking about our kids. It took that relationship to the next level, and right away I noticed that her associates started being a little nicer to me. She is well respected there, and I think they assumed that if she liked me, I must be all right. I would not have expected this turn of events when I started working with this account three years ago, but in the end, I might have gained their trust by being consistent and professional, even when I wasn't winning their business, and I might even turn a business relationship into a friendship.

Just as happy dogs will lick your face to show that they love you, happy customers will keep coming back to buy more from you, or your company. Who doesn't love more slobber on your face and more sales?

CHAPTER FIVE

Gotta Go Now!

CUSTOMER URGENCY

H ere's the thing about sales: It's not about your timeline, it's about your customers' timelines. It doesn't matter to them that it's the end of your fiscal year and you are at 99.4 percent of your quota and their order would put you at 100 percent, especially after you busted your tail off. What matters to them . . . is what matters to them. Remember, it's not about you, it's about them. The sooner you realize that, the better you will be at sales.

It's like dogs: When they have to go, they have to go. At the dog park or on a walk, they go right then and there. When dogs are in the house and need to go, they will bark, whine, or scratch on the door to tell you so. If ignored, they will go on the floor or carpet because they "gotta go now." As a dog owner, you need to learn how long your dog can hold it and work backwards from that to figure how long your dog can be left alone. If your dog needs to go every two hours but you have to be out of the house for four hours, you better have a doggy door or dog walker lined up or you are going to come home to an oops on the floor. That's just the life of a dog owner.

You need to figure out what is urgent to your customers and learn to reframe what is important to you so that what you do helps them. Most don't care that you are at 99.4 percent of your quota, although a couple of great customers might. As much as you want to tell them you need their help, don't do it. You don't want them to think you are coming to them to force a sale so you can reach your quota. Remember, a key to sales is about reframing what is important to you into something that is important to your client.

We all have the "gotta go now" customers who need everything immediately, even when they don't. Part of the role of a salesperson is to figure out if these are real deadlines or not. If a customer is asking how long it takes to order and ship products, you can try to turn it around by asking something like, "Can you please walk me through your implementation timeline so we can work backwards from when you need the product to determine when you would need to order?" I've asked clients directly if they truly need it in two days. In those cases, I present them with a realistic schedule. Often, they just want to order it quickly to get it off their plate, or they may think it will take longer to get there than it actually does.

If it's a product that has to ship, they are not going to get it tomorrow, unless they are ordering on Amazon. (In that case, what do they need you for?) If you have identified that they just have a hair-on-fire mentality, you can often assuage their fears (whether they be real or imagined) by talking about the ways you can help them get the order placed quickly. Is there a way you can speed up the order process? Can they send it to you directly this one time so you can push the order through? Can you give the warehouse a heads-up that it's coming so they can turn it around quickly?

If you have asked several probing questions about why they need it so quickly and you realize their urgency is based on a real deadline that you cannot meet, it may mean being honest with them and resetting their expectations. If they really "gotta have it now!" and you can't accommodate that, chances are neither can your competition, so the customer will have to change their deadline or not order the product at that time. If you handle the situation with honesty and professionalism, they may still come back to you for future orders.

If their deadline is real and you can't meet it, you may have to say something difficult such as, "As much as I'd love to help you and have your order that product from us, I just don't want to set unrealistic expectations of when you are going to get the product. I don't think we will be able to hit your deadline, so you may need to look elsewhere." And if you are really customer-service oriented you may add, "I can give you the names of a few of our competitors I trust, and you can see if they can get it to you in time." Chances are if they are being unrealistic about deadlines, your competitors can't help them either, but they will remember the salesperson who was honest and gave them advice on where else they could order it.

FIGURE OUT THE CUSTOMER TIMELINE UP FRONT SO THERE ARE NO SURPRISES

As mentioned, the first thing you need to find out is what their timeline is for the purchase. I ask that up front and have found that most prospects are happy to tell you their timeline, if you ask. If it's a business-to-business (B2B) situation, you might get a short answer like the end of the year. (Make sure you clarify if they are on a fiscal or calendar year and, if fiscal, when their end of year is exactly.) Sometimes you get a more personal answer, such as, "I'm saving up my money working a second job at Kmart every other Tuesday from 7 to 10 p.m. to buy this product."

Once you determine what their timeline is, you need to ask their budget and the status of the funds needed. Knowing their timeline helps you with the framing of the rest of the conversation. "I need it today" is a much different sales conversation then, "I'm hoping to be able to afford this in the next year or two." I find it's easier to ask their timeline and budget in a B2B sale because it's not personal. Next, I'll ask if their funds have already been allocated. This should be a simple yes or no answer. I try my best to follow that up with a question about how much has been allocated for the purchase. If they are willing to answer these questions, I ask if they are the decision-maker. If the answer is no, then I ask who is. This information is the golden ticket. You'll now know

(1) their timeframe, (2) if there are funds to purchase, (3) how much they are hoping to spend, and (4) who makes the decision.

I wish I could say that I always have this information up front, but I either don't always ask or the prospect doesn't want to tell me. Both of those are OK. If you forget to ask up front, you can always ask later with such questions as: "I can't remember when you said you are looking to make this purchase. Can you remind me?" "I forgot if these funds have already been allocated or not. Could you remind me?" "What is the amount that you are looking to spend?" or, "Can you remind me if you are the decision-maker on this purchase?" A word of caution: if the prospect does not want to divulge information about their budget, etc., be careful not to push. You don't want to be known as a pushy salesperson; you want to be known as a trusted advisor.

When I want to see what the status of a possible order is, instead of asking when the customer is going to send the PO, I say something like, "I know you wanted to get that curriculum before school starts, so you will need to get the PO to me by July 1 to do that. Is that something you can do?" That shows that (1) you heard them say that they want or need to get the product by a certain date, (2) you are letting them know how much lead time you need to hit their deadline, and (3) you are not asking to meet your needs but are trying to meet their needs.

Predicting the status of an order and if and when it will come in is called forecasting. Let's face it, we all want to be able to predict when an order is going to come in and hit our quota, but it's easier said than done. Not only do we have to get the correct information from our customers, we have to get it to our management, and we want our management to see us as the experts on what is coming in and when. Your manager has to roll up to upper management, and, if it's a public company, the CEO needs to know whether the company is going to meet or exceed the revenue that they publicly committed to. The better you can be at forecasting, the better your boss can be, and your boss's boss, and the happier your boss and boss's boss will be with you. It all goes back to what my dad said about making sure your boss and boss's boss are happy. Of course you want the company to thrive and the CEO to be successful, but the most important people to you and your career are your boss and your boss's boss.

It's also important as a salesperson to know what sales are coming in and when, which is called managing your pipeline. I have to work hard to put time aside to clean up my pipeline because I get busy doing other things and it's often hard to give it priority. In full disclosure, it's usually a few days before a meeting with management in which we'll review my pipeline that I kick into high gear. If I don't put enough time aside, it becomes the speed dating of pipeline management. I might have to go through up to one hundred opportunities to make sure I have the right close date, percentage of whether they will close, pipeline status, and so forth. It's much easier if you do it consistently, but this is one of those "do what I say and not what I do" areas.

Besides managing your pipeline, your boss may ask you to continuously forecast what you expect to bring in for the quarter or the remainder of the year. That means you have to look at your pipeline and give your best guess on how much revenue you will bring in during a certain period of time (usually a month, quarter, current year, or future year). One time I did not do a great job of forecasting my anticipated quarterly revenue and my boss had to readjust her forecast to her boss because of it. She was upset with me because she did not look good to her boss. Again, it goes back to bosses and bosses' bosses.

After that, I concocted this really complicated formula of figuring out my monthly forecast. I forecasted my leads in three main buckets: (1) the ones I felt the least confident about, I forecasted between a 1–25 percent likelihood they would close; (2) the ones I was 50/50 as to whether they would close, I forecasted between 30–70 percent; and (3) the ones I felt confident would close, I forecasted between 80–90 percent. I really put thought into what the chances of closing were in each bucket of my forecasted numbers. I then weighted each one a certain percentage based on the probability that it would close, and I made it so complicated that I won't give any more detail because it hurts my head just thinking about it.

After doing this for about six months, I realized that my associates who put almost no thought into their forecast and just took a guess with 50 percent of their total pipeline were coming in close to my estimates and that I was wasting time with my overly complicated formula.

It was a good reminder that sometimes the most complicated solution is just more complicated and not necessarily more accurate. Still, in order to avoid overestimating your forecasted revenue, you need to come up with some method of forecasting and put some time into it.

In my current role at the same company, we have all agreed on the general rule that you need four to five times your quota in your pipeline at the beginning of the year to hit your annual quota. So if you need to bring in $25 million in a year, you are going to need to start the year with $100–$125 million in potential business. As the year moves on, we put the rest into two buckets—committed and forecasted—and say that we expect to bring in 100 percent of anything that has been verbally committed to and anywhere from 25–50 percent of the rest of your pipeline. (You can adjust in that range easily by looking at your pipeline to see which of the biggest opportunities are real or not. Remember: no one is more of an expert than you.)

There are times when your dog just really has "gotta go." It may be a pain, but you can't ignore it. You need to act quickly to prevent a much bigger problem. With your customers, do the same. Have a plan in place and apply it to those (hopefully) rare times when you need to switch to high gear and put out a fire immediately.

Oops!

MISTAKES WILL HAPPEN: CLEAN THEM UP QUICKLY
AND WITHOUT ANGER

We all know mistakes happen. It's how you handle them that shows your character. I'm as guilty as the next person of wanting to sweep mistakes under the rug and hope no one notices them. Something I have to work on every day is to admit when a mistake happened or try to get ahead of something that I know is going to go wrong and figure out a plan before it's too late.

Dogs make mistakes, too. We all know that having a puppy means that there will be lots of oops moments. When your dog gets older, they have less mistakes, but just like in life, mistakes will continue to happen. You can either spend your time and energy getting angry about the mistake your dog made, or you can clean it up and move on. You also have to try to get better about anticipating them. For instance, if I leave my dog inside for four hours and don't have a plan to let him outside to relieve himself, he is going to have an accident. So, if I know we are going to be out all day, we have to make a plan, which usually involves paying someone to take him out but that is part of the cost of dog ownership.

One time we wanted to go on a hike as a family, but the hike was one hour away. We knew we were pushing it by leaving Oliver alone for four hours, but we couldn't find anyone to let him out. When we came home, we discovered a nice surprise at the top of the stairs from him. We couldn't get too mad because we knew better than to leave him that long, so we just cleaned it up and made sure to plan better next time.

When you make a mistake as a salesperson, you also need to deal with it quickly and efficiently. We all make mistakes. The best way of handling them is to admit when you are to blame, take responsibility, and fix the issue. It goes back to building trust and long-term relationships. If the mistake negatively affects the customer, do what you can to minimize the pain they will feel because of your mistake.

I recently forgot to send a customer some sample products I promised her. When she asked about it, I admitted that I hadn't done it and expedited the order so it would get there around the same time it would have originally gotten there. By expediting it, I did cost the company extra money but I salvaged a relationship, and I will trim costs in other places to make up for the expedited shipping cost. When you make a mistake, simply admit that you made a mistake and fix it if you can with what is in your power to do so. Don't pass the blame or get angry about it. When you lie about a mistake or don't take responsibility, customers will see a pattern and you will lose their trust.

Often in a company someone else makes a mistake but you get the blame because you're in the customer-facing role. I can't even count the number of times that customers have gotten angry at me for mistakes that someone else in my company made. When that happens, I let them vent and then I try to fix the problem as soon as possible without taking it personally or overly explaining that it was not me who made the mistake.

Sometimes it does get under my skin when customers lash out at me just because they can when I didn't do anything wrong. If I am working from home that day, I have to take a fifteen-minute break to walk my dog around the block, load the dishwasher, or fix a snack in order to calm down.

HOW YOU HANDLE MISTAKES IS MORE IMPORTANT THAN THE MISTAKE ITSELF

As mentioned, it's often not the mistake but how you fix it that matters. I remember a time recently when a customer needed to have samples of a product before a big meeting to show our product in contrast to a few competitors. I decided to save the time of shipping it from our warehouse by having someone on my team drop it off in person as we had some extras in a local storage unit.

I called the customer a few days before the meeting to make sure she had received them and she informed me that we had dropped off the wrong product that had a similar name. I apologized and said that I would drop off the correct product the next day. I personally went and found the product that she needed in the storage unit and dropped it off myself. I made sure to drop it off directly to the customer and apologize to her as opposed to just leaving it at the front desk. It took a few hours out of my day to do it myself, but I wanted to let her know that it was important to me that we fixed our mistake. I think she was so impressed that I fixed the problem the next day (and that I dropped it off myself) that we made the short list of products for them to evaluate.

There have been other times when I have not handled mistakes as well as I would have liked. I usually keep my cool, but a couple of times when I've had an upset customer taking it out on me, I've responded with a snippy sentence like, "The shipping department made the mistake, and I'm trying everything I can do to fix it for you so please cut me some slack." That situation usually ends up with both of us apologizing and realizing we were both out of line.

Being honest when the mistake was yours, not over-explaining when it wasn't, letting your customers vent to you if that's what they need to do, and then doing your best to fix the mistake goes a long way with customers in building their long-term trust.

We are all going to have oops moments with our customers and with our dogs, so just make sure you clean it up quickly without getting angry or getting your fur in a bunch.

CHAPTER SEVEN

A Chow Chow Is Not a Lab Is Not a Beagle

LET THEM TELL YOU WHAT'S IMPORTANT TO THEM BEFORE DIVING INTO YOUR SALES PITCH

I know a woman who hadn't had a lot of experience with dogs and adopted a one-year-old Chow Chow. She took her dog to the dog park expecting it to play fetch with her. But when she threw the ball, more often than not, her dog didn't respond. Occasionally, her dog ran after the ball but never once retrieved it. But here's the thing: Chows are not retrievers. (She was also surprised by the intensity of her dog's protective instincts, but she was able to manage those with training and socialization.) Years later, after her dog passed away, she adopted a new dog, a Lab mix. She took the dog to the backyard and, without thinking, tossed a ball. Her new Lab ran after the ball, picked it up, and brought it back to her—at nine weeks old with no training. So you see, a Chow Chow is not a Lab. Your prospects and customers are the same. They are not one-size-fits all, so neither should your sales pitch be.

We've all been there. We have a preplanned sales pitch or a forty-slide deck PowerPoint presentation to present to our prospect to get a sale. We may have worked on the presentation for weeks getting the slides to look perfect and the graphics to move on the slides, and we are ready to close this deal. We arrive at the presentation with guns blazing, and after quick introductions, dive right into the presentation. We don't stop to take a breath as we go over our perfectly polished one-sided presentation. Ever been there and done that? I have, many times. Sometimes we get so excited about what we are selling or our presentation that we forget to ask what the customers need or want and what is important to them.

In my current sales role, I see this phenomenon from another vantage point. I get to bring in Curriculum Specialists, who do the actual presentations, so I'm not usually the one presenting. Even though I don't actually do the product demo or presentation, I have spent countless hours beforehand cultivating the relationship and getting our foot in the door.

The best presentations I've seen are the ones where the presenter is confident enough to begin the presentation with questions about what the customer is looking for. It takes a seasoned presenter to do this because it could change the course of the presentation. You may even have to skip some slides—even the brilliant ones that took hours to create—but you will get to the heart of what the customer wants. (Think of throwing a ball for a Chow Chow.) The presenter may ask what the top one or two things the client is hoping to get out of the presentation, or what their customers complain about most and how we can change that. These are the hot buttons for the client. You can weave the answers into your talk even if you don't have a fancy PowerPoint slide that matches word for word.

Another way to figure out what is important to the customer is to ask them some questions in advance of the meeting. I've done this with a brief in-person pre-meeting, over the phone, or by email. As a side note, I try to make sure every time I'm in front of the customer, they leave thinking it was worth their time. You can skip this pre-meeting, but I find there are usually one or two things they mention that I had not anticipated, which, as a result, I can address in the presentation. (You may even look like you read their mind.) I prefer to meet with my contact in person before bringing in anyone else from my company to present. I can ask candid questions about their needs and pain points so that we make sure to address those in the presentation.

When you ask your prospect about what is important to them, price will almost always be mentioned as the most important issue. Just remember that anyone who has ever negotiated any deal knows that you always bring up price up front. If not, you may pay more than you should as there is usually room for negotiation. So, price will probably be mentioned, but often it's not always about price but about the value that they are receiving. Maybe they need to implement right away so the purchasing or shipping time frame is important. Now that you know that, you can set expectations for what to expect once the order is placed. Maybe they have less space in their warehouse or store, so the size or shape of packaging or having "just in time" inventory is key. You may not have anticipated these questions, but now you can be prepared for them and possibly even bring an expert from packaging, inventory, or shipping to the meeting to directly address their issues.

This approach also means you'll have to get to know your prospects' and customers' unique culture and business models. One of my most memorable customers was a large warehouse club. I was working at a well-known software company in Silicon Valley and we did so much business with it that it was my only customer. I had to completely rethink how I worked with customers. In the past, the customers had appreciated the value-add of developing a relationship with me (their vendor) to make business more personal and, honestly, more fun. This customer was sometimes challenging to work with as it kept all of their vendors at arm's length. The warehouse felt strongly about keeping a distance from the vendors and not forming tight relationships so it didn't show favoritism. That way, it was able to keep their vendor relationships neutral and could switch from one vendor to another if a vendor didn't provide the high value that it expects.

It might have made their job easier to keep the vendors at an arm's length. For me, it was tough because I couldn't make personal connections with my contacts, which made it harder to differentiate ourselves from the competition and its salespeople. I'd ask the corporate folks if they would like to go to lunch or dinner after an upcoming meeting and they always politely turned me down. I couldn't forge real relationships with my only customer account at the time. I did gain a lot of respect for them, as all of the employees were extremely dedicated to their company and focused on getting the best value for their customers, whom they called members because it was a warehouse club with a paid membership.

If you have never shopped at a warehouse club, just imagine a huge warehouse that has no frills where you buy most everything in bulk at a great value. It has a 'treasure hunt' mentality where it rotates products in prime space so you never know what you'll find, and that keeps members coming back often to see what it has in stock. You could find winter coats one week or diamond rings the next. It doesn't even give you grocery bags; it puts your items in boxes that it gets from its vendors. What a great way to recycle! The warehouse spends a lot of time narrowing each category to the products it thinks represent the best one or two brands and then negotiate like crazy with those vendors to get the best pricing so that you as a member can feel confident you're getting the best deal.

The first thing I had to learn as its vendor was to change all my terminology from stores to warehouses and customers to members. Everything it does is about getting a better value for its members, which was the next thing I had to learn. It actually had maximum margins that it could make from products so that most of the savings went straight to reducing the price for the member. Let me say that again, it limited the margin that it would make on products so that its members could get better pricing. The warehouse was a tough negotiator, but it was not trying to make more money for the company but to get better pricing for its members. It was obsessive about getting its members the best value, and I respected the warehouse for that.

As mentioned, my contacts at the warehouse club didn't want to be wined and dined, and they wouldn't even go to lunch with me after a meeting at their corporate offices. (We were a pretty big vendor to them.) As one of the vendors, I had to rethink everything I said or presented to them around member value. They were not interested in special deals unless it could be passed on to their members. They cared about packaging in terms of how the product was shipped to the warehouse and what shape and size it was to make the most of their shelf space. I remember them telling me how they asked their milk vendor to change from a regular milk jug to a square milk jug because it would fit more efficiency in their refrigerated section. And the vendor did make that change for them because the warehouse is such a large retailer, and the vendor knew it would have been kicked out of the warehouse if it hadn't done so.

It was a good reminder that we should always be thinking about how we can help our customers and make their lives easier. When you truly have a customer-first mindset it will shine through, and your customers will stop treating you like a salesperson and more of a trusted partner. This experience also taught me that some of the lessons I'd learned in the past didn't apply to this particular customer. A one-size-fits-all approach wouldn't work, and once I learned that, I had a much more fruitful relationship with my customer—just like my acquaintance had a much better relationship with her dog once she understood its unique temperament.

CHAPTER EIGHT

Fetch (Again and Again)

CONTINUOUS CUSTOMER CONTACT IS KEY

Do you ever watch a dog fetch and retrieve a ball over and over again and think, "Doesn't that get boring?" If you know dogs, you know that some of them are just plain ball obsessed. These dogs don't care about other dogs as much as they care about their ball. And they can chase it over and over again without getting bored.

It's like customer contact in sales. You have to fetch and retrieve over and over again to get the results that you want. You may have some lucky times where you get a sale without doing much or any of the work (it's called a bluebird in sales), but those are few and far between. Sometimes it looks to others as though we got a bluebird as the sale seemingly came out of nowhere when in fact you did work at some point in the past with that prospect or customer to get what appears to be an easy sale now. We all wish we could have bluebirds all of the time to help us easily hit our quotas so we could sit back with wine, chai tea, or a vanilla latte (insert your drink of choice) and watch the sales roll in. Of course, that is unrealistic and will never happen, but, like buying a lottery ticket, it's fun to imagine what you'd do with the money if you picked the winning numbers.

Sales requires a lot of hard work, and part of that work is continuous customer contact. You can't expect prospects or customers to buy from you after reaching out to them just one time. The marketing team will tell you that you need to reach out to the customer in different ways multiple times to get them to respond to any advertising.

Different marketers cite different numbers for different industries, but let's say you need to contact prospects and customers five to twelve times before they purchase. I think most people use the Rule of Seven (i.e., it takes seven times to get a customer to respond). Just as the marketers know it takes multiple contacts to get a response, in sales we know that to build relationships and to make sales, you have to follow up with the prospect or customer time and time again (remember the dog fetching and retrieving the ball?). The follow-up should occur both when they are looking to buy and when they are not. (Although you want to follow up more frequently when they are actively looking, you still want to be on their radar when they are not.) It is challenging as a salesperson to figure out the right timing and number of times to reach out to prospects or customers, and you just need to keep adjusting until you figure out what works for you.

I don't have a hard and fast rule about it, but here is a formula that I have used. I divide up my prospects and customers into four buckets: (1) The hot group—those who might purchase in the next few months, (2); the warm group—those who might purchase in the next six months to a year, (3); the cool group—those who might purchase sometime in the long term;, and (4) the cold group—the tire kickers who I know can't afford to purchase or who have wasted my time in the past and never purchased. I try to have some communication with the hot group weekly, the warm group monthly, the cool group quarterly, and the cold group semi-annually (or not at all if I know from experience it won't purchase and will only waste my time).

Sometimes you get customers who say they need or want to buy in the next week or month, so you create a special group called the red hot group and reach out to them as much as appropriate. Daily? Twice a week? You need to figure out what is appropriate for your business setting. Remember the goal, other than to get the sale, is to move them up through the groups, i.e., to get those in the cool and warm groups to move up to the hot groups. You might reach out to someone in the cool group who was going to purchase in the next year and find out they have extra funds they need to spend in the next month or they will lose them, so you move them straight up to the red hot group and act accordingly.

Another nuance in sales—and something that is easier to do with relationship-based versus transactional sales—is figuring out how best to reach out to different customers. If you have been working in the same role for years with the same repeat customers, you may know that Bob from Company W likes to talk on the phone, Mary from Company X likes to communicate by email, Jose from Company Y likes you to stop by in person, and Ralph from Company Z only likes you to send flyers in the mail. If you are able to figure out how someone likes to communicate and be consistent in communicating that way, you will have more success.

I was working a big deal a couple of years ago with a large school district and couldn't always get in touch with my main contact when I needed to. I'd email her or leave her a voice message at work and only heard back from her if it was something she wanted to talk to me about. This made it difficult to provide information in a timely manner to my team and management on this potential multimillion dollar sale.

One day I tried her on her cell at about 7:30 in the morning and reached her during her commute to work. She was happy to talk, and I soon realized that she drove to work at the same time every morning for about forty-five minutes and was always happy to talk at that time. Learning that nugget really helped my communications with her and enabled me to get information back to my team and management in a timely manner. We ended up closing the deal, and my contact and I had a good relationship because most of our calls happened before she was in her cubicle at the district office, so she was more open with me—and she was quite chatty since she was driving for forty-five minutes and wanted to pass the time.

CONTINUE TO MARKET TO THE SAME GROUP

Another thing to remember about continuous customer contact is not to forget to go back to your current and, hopefully, happy customers to see if they need anything else from you. This practice is either called cross-selling or upselling, but those words always sound so impersonal to me, so I just think of it as finding more opportunities with existing customers. If someone buys your product and you move on to the next prospect or customer without following up to see if there is anything else in your portfolio they might want or need post-sale, you have lost out on an opportunity for another sale (which will be much easier than the first sale as you have already invested time and energy into the relationship).

None of this has to take a lot of time. I like to borrow and repurpose to save time, so I often create what looks like a personalized email that I send out to multiple customers with only a little customization. What I do is make the title of the email and the body of the email the same so that I can quickly copy the email, change the person's name, and customize it to their company or school district. In this way, I can send a lot of emails in a short time, taking about one minute each to customize it.

Here's an example of a short thank-you note that you can easily repurpose by inserting the person's name and the company (or school district in this example) where I have X and Y:

> *Thank you so much for your recent purchase. We are so happy that School District Y has decided to adopt our*

social science products. I hope that you find that our product exceeds your needs.

If you have any questions on setting up the product, please contact customer service at 800-888-8888. If you have any other questions or would like any additional products or services, please contact me directly at 888-111-1212.

Again, thank you for the purchase and we appreciate your business.

Sincerely,

[Add email signature with your contact information]

The email looks personal, but really, it's a template that you can use over and over again with different customers. I actually create a template with the X in there so that I can just do a search on X (on my Mac, I just do a Command + F and put X) to find all of the places I need to customize, so it really does take a minute or less to send a personalized email.

When you think about cross-selling or upselling, think of Amazon. When you're looking to buy something from it, it provides you with a list of items you may want, whether as deals of the day, items related to ones you have viewed, or more items to explore. It is smart. It is cross-selling and upselling all of the time. It knows you may want or need other items besides the one or two (or ten) items you went there to purchase. You don't have to be as obvious as Amazon because you are taking a more hands-on approach of talking, emailing, and so forth with your customers while Amazon is trying to sell you as much as it can every time you go onto its site without any real customer contact. It has such advanced algorithms, it seems to read your mind about what you might want to buy (scary, I know, but I'm still a devoted Amazon shopper). Let's pretend you are a salesperson for a Mom and Pop office store. You can contact an existing customer and say, "Hi, X. I know you recently bought a printer from us. Are you happy with it? I see you didn't buy a warranty, are you interested in purchasing that now? Do you need any paper, extra printer cartridges, or anything else for your office? We have a full array of office supplies that we can help you with." You can follow up with a customer and find out if they need something else from you at the same time.

Let's say you can make an extra 10 percent on selling additional products or services to existing customers. If you have a quota of $1 million, that's $100,000 that you can get from selling more to existing customers. It will be a lot easier to make that $100,000 from existing customers than if you had to find new prospects and cultivate relationships to try to sell $100,000. We often forget to go back to our existing customers to make more sales. It's the easiest way to sell but we often forget to look at this low-hanging fruit.

Think of it like teaching your dog new tricks versus getting a new dog and trying to train them on everything. Sometimes training your existing dog to do something new is still time consuming and certainly not as exciting as getting a new dog, but it's usually easier than starting at square one with a dog that doesn't know you or your style.

You need to remember to continue to contact existing customers for more business just as you have to throw the ball to your dog over and over again at the dog park. Even if you find it repetitive and boring, your dog won't and your constant customer contact may be just what is needed to get another sale. Sometimes you don't get anything out of the repetition and it seems an exercise in futility, but it's still easier than finding a new customer— or trying to train a new dog.

CHAPTER NINE

Roll Down the Window and Take in the Smells

IF YOU'RE PASSIONATE ABOUT YOUR PRODUCT OR SERVICE, IT WILL SHOW

Most of us have had sales jobs that we were not passionate about and, hopefully, didn't have to do long term. We should be more like dogs and sniff out situations. We humans often forget to roll down the window and take in the smells. Dogs do a great job of being attuned to their surroundings and can tell whether a smell is good or bad or another dog is good or bad right away.

Most of us have had jobs that we didn't love, were not passionate about, or even hated, but sometimes we bury our heads in the sand, not realizing it's obvious to others that we're not happy. If only we took a good whiff and just admitted it smells bad, it would save us a lot of time and stress. And if you are selling a product that you don't love or work for a company that you don't believe in, it may be obvious to everyone but you. Sometimes you need to step back and take stock of your job and know when it's time to go. I know it's not always possible to leave a job. That terrible job may be the best, or only, way to put food on the table. In most cases, you don't need to quit your job right away; however, you can make a plan to change jobs and work backwards from it like we talked about in chapter 1 on changing jobs.

If you're unhappy in your job, think about what would make you happy before you make any changes. The worst thing to do would be to leave one bad job for another bad one. You have to spend a lot of time and energy to change jobs, so make sure you don't do it before putting thought into what you are giving up versus what you are getting. I don't believe in doing a lateral move unless there is something at the new job that is better than the last (e.g., stock options, better company culture, or better future opportunities).

Here is a trick I learned from a business podcast and then customized, so it's a little bit borrowed and a little bit mine. Get a blank piece of paper or open a new doc and create three boxes: (1) skills you have and would enjoy using; (2) skills you have but don't enjoy using; and (3) skills you don't have but would be willing or happy to learn. You know you could do what's in box 2, but you don't want to spend your precious time doing things that don't give you positive energy, so ignore box 2. That's right, even though they are skills you have, they are skills you don't enjoy using, so ignore them. You want this next job to be better than the current job and . . . you want to be happy.

Look at boxes 1 and 3. If things in boxes 1 and 3 align

to what you are doing now but you don't like the company or the product, look for a similar job with a company or product line that you are passionate about. If those skills have nothing to do with what you are doing now, you need to do some serious reflecting and research about what it would take to change your career to do something you would love. Just make sure you are willing to put in the required effort.

If you realize you don't like sales anymore, then learn something new or dust off some skills you used in a prior job and get looking for a job. I'm a believer in side hustles, so I think you can spend some time outside of work to learn new skills or start up a side business without quitting your day job until you are financially ready to do so. You can make a one-to-three year plan to learn new skills on the side to transition to a new career (you can call it your exit strategy if you want it to sound fancy).

On the flip side, if you love your job and are passionate about your company and/or product, you probably should stay where you are. Hopefully that passion shines through and you are selling tons and knocking it out of the ballpark. If you think there is room for improvement where you are, see if you need more from your current company (e.g., more products, more training, better commission structure, or more resources or support) and don't be afraid to ask for it. Take the time to evaluate yourself honestly, figure out if there is something else you can do in the next year or so to be both happier and more successful in your current job, think of all of the things you need to do to get there and then get moving.

Too many people stay at bad jobs or dead-end jobs due to inertia. Don't be that person. That person is boring at parties. They usually complain about a job they never loved or just say their job is "fine" without sharing anything positive about it. You don't want to be that person. You want to be the one who is so excited about your job that your excitement attracts others to you. It's like my dog, Oliver. When he arrives at the dog park, he is all about fun and playing with all of the other dogs, and I like to say the party starts when he arrives.

NOTICE CUSTOMER SIGNALS ALONG THE WAY AND BE PREPARED TO GO OFF TRACK

As well as thinking about your own happiness and health (and not being the wet rag at parties), you need to constantly evaluate your customer relationships to see how healthy they are. If you know that things can be better, be ready to go off track when needed. By that, I mean if you notice a customer hasn't been contacting you as much as usual or you see they are carrying a different product, you need to repair the relationship. If you think you are losing traction in any way with a customer, get in there quick to fix it. Remember that if you aren't in there, your competitors are.

I suggest an in-person meeting in order to probe and figure out what is going on. Do you not have the right products? Did you not deliver the product or service at the right time? Was the price higher than you said it would be? Did your customer not get superior customer service? Did the other salesperson have a nicer Power-Point presentation than you (just kidding!)? You'll never know what the issue is unless you ask and listen. Listen carefully and continue to probe if you don't think they are telling you the real reason for breaking up with you. Note that if your customer says your price is too high, that's similar to someone ending a relationship with, "It's not you, it's me." Most often, it is an easy excuse people use when something else is wrong (both in your business and the relationship) and they don't want to take the time or effort to tell you what it is.

You'll need to probe further if you want to know the truth. But only probe if you are willing to hear the truth and also willing to make changes to save the relationship. Set the expectations for the in-person meeting by telling them that you'd like to have a business review and are not trying to sell them anything. If you have data to show product usage, purchasing patterns, return on investment, click rate, or whatever data is relevant to your business line and the customer would find helpful, it will give you the opportunity to review the business objectively, ask questions, and share any exciting new products or news that you have.

Sometimes these meetings are going to be high level where you bring in management from both sides and sometimes it can be just you and your main contact at the organization. My personal opinion is to try to make this a casual one-on-one with your customer only. I find I get more feedback and the "real scoop" if it's just my contact and me. But sometimes you need to bring in your posse from the office (including the "big dogs") to show them how important they are to your company or to get important decisions made that you or your contact couldn't make on the spot. You need to decide what is appropriate, a one-on-one meeting with your contact or bringing in your posse for a dog and pony show as it's called in sales (e.g., big presentation, bringing in the higher-ups, and so forth). Either way, most likely something went off track in the relationship, and first you need to figure out what went wrong and then whether you can fix it.

One thing that I have done and found effective is have the meeting first with your contact and see if you can get buy-in from them to have the bigger meeting so that the two of you can be on the same page when you bring your higher-ups together. I just did that with my largest customer a few months ago. I met with my contact and hammered out some issues, and then when we met with the higher-ups, we had jointly developed an agenda. At several points my contact said, "Julie and I discussed that and we thought. . . ." I couldn't have paid her to sound more collaborative, and it made me look great to my management team. And as I've said before, the two most important people in our careers are our boss and our boss's boss.

If you are able to figure out how the relationship went off track or if a new company swooped in with better products or a better deal, you need to be prepared to fix what went wrong. Was price really the issue and not just an excuse? Could you come up with a pricing situation based on volume, bundling multiple products, or being their only supplier (a sole-supplier or sole-source relationship) that makes you unique and more valuable than your competition? This is where you need to be creative to save a relationship and realize that money is not always the answer.

Maybe it was a big account that didn't feel like they were getting enough support from your company. Can you revamp the way you handle that customer, e.g., put more resources towards that account, such as a dedicated sales and/or marketing person, or take the account from an inside salesperson who sits in a cubicle in another state and put it under a field salesperson who could visit them in person? Make sure you are reading your customer signals (good and bad) and can react when you need to make changes about how you work with the customer in order to save the relationship.

Like your dog, learn to quickly assess when a sales position or a relationship no longer smells good. Make sure you are attuned to the signals your customer is sending you and be prepared to go off track if necessary. It's hard to hide a bad smell if you are taking the time to sniff the air, so don't forget to roll down the window and take in the smells, decide if they are good or bad, and then adjust your relationship accordingly.

CHAPTER TEN

I'm Not Going in There: the Vet

CHECKUPS AND CHECK-INS ARE IMPORTANT
TO THE HEALTH OF ANY RELATIONSHIP

Whose dog loves going to the vet? I feel like there may be a joke in here. "What do going to the vet and running into a mean dog at the dog park have in common?" "They both bite." Once Oliver wised up about the vet, he would refuse to get out of the car when we arrived. One time I had to lift him on the ground and coax him to come inside—he's a seventy-pound dog, so it wasn't easy to do. But even if your dog hates the vet, it necessary to go in order to keep your dog healthy and catch any health or behavior problems before they get to be too bad.

It's the same with any relationship, so you can apply this advice to both your personal and business relationships. You need constant check-ins to fix problems (in good times and in bad) when the problems are still little to not let them get so far out of control that the relationship is too far gone to save. I know for myself, I am often so focused on turning tangible current opportunities into future revenue that I don't always take the time to think about nurturing the relationships with customers who might not be actively looking to buy but are important just the same.

I try to remember to do this by reaching out to customers in person, on the phone, or by email and asking how things are going, if they are happy with the product or service I sold them, and what their current needs or challenges are. Checking in when you are not trying to sell them something strengthens the relationship, and by hearing their current needs, you may be able to help them with a problem they didn't realize you have a solution for.

All salespeople follow up post-sale in their own way. I don't think there is a magic formula. You need to figure out what works for you. Maybe you like to write a handwritten thank you note after a purchase or call thirty days after the purchase to make sure everything is working the way it should or be able to run interference to make it better if there is an issue.

Someone at the dog park was telling me recently that she ordered her dog food from www.chewy.com. It was set up on a set delivery schedule, and when her dog died, she called to cancel the delivery. Soon after, she received a sympathy note in the mail. She said that that extra effort made her feel like they cared about her and her dog, and she will be sure to use them for her next dog. That's an example of going that extra mile to show your customers that you are grateful for their business and that you care. Most of us are not going to write sympathy notes when our customers' dogs die (nor should we or that might be a little creepy), but it is appropriate to get one from your dog food delivery company. Take some time to think of what you can do to let your customers know you are thinking about them in a non-creepy way.

As we all know, if you let a situation fester or if you stumble across a customer that wasn't happy about something you did or the product you sold them and you never bothered to follow up with them, you could be stepping into a land mine. At that point, it may be too late to fix the relationship, but if you had made an effort to check in when there wasn't the opportunity for a sale, you could have saved that customer relationship, and then they might think of you the next time they need something. Sadly, because you didn't make an effort to check in when there was not a new sale to be had, that customer will probably go to a competitor, possibly tell several friends or associates about their bad experience with you and your company, and you may lose several customers as a result. Make sure you make the extra effort to check in with your customers even when you may not get a sale because it's the right thing to do, and you may save a relationship that you didn't even know had soured.

USE DASHBOARDS TO MEASURE YOUR PROGRESS AND SEE WHERE YOU NEED TO PUT MORE ATTENTION

One practice that I adopted while working in Silicon Valley was to create a dashboard about more important relationships. This will not be appropriate for all people reading this (i.e., it might not make sense if you are doing transactional sales and the customer only buys from you once), but those of us in relationship sales need to keep an eye on the status of the relationship and know when to course correct. If you have a lot of customers like I do, you may just do it for the top 10 percent of your customers based on strategic importance and/or revenue. Dashboards can be used in a variety of ways to check the health of the relationship. Here is one method I use with large strategic relationships.

Divide a paper (or PowerPoint) into two sections. The first section is for learnings. You list the learnings about the customer and then list the implication of those learnings. It could be anything, but an example might be that you are selling holiday lights to retail stores and released a revolutionary product for the holiday season. A learning might be, "We released our new product on November 1, and the customer said it was too late for them to buy the product for that season." The implication might be, "We lost the business because we didn't understand the customer timeline. They needed the new product in their warehouse by October 1 to get it into their stores for their holiday season."

The second section is the scorecard. This section is a visual and an easy way to assess the health of the relationship. I like to use red, yellow, and green colors so that it looks like a stoplight and you can quickly see where you need to make changes or improvements. Come up with concrete things you are trying to measure about the relationship. The first half can measure the health of the relationship and the second half can measure whether the salesperson has all of the products and tools that he or she needed to make a sale. Some measurements under the health of the relationship include (1) whether you're on track to meet your customer quota; (2) year-over-year growth; and (3) customer satisfaction. Some measurements under customer tools include (1) whether you have the right products, (2) whether you have the authority to make decisions and give discounts, and (3) whether you have the right add-on products for additional sales. Next to all of these, you would put a green, yellow, or red circle or box to show the health of the relationship (green means everything is fine, yellow means there may be an issue and this area needs some attention, and red means that something is seriously wrong and this area needs attention ASAP).

I have always liked this stoplight visual. You can also add a dashboard with a list of questions (say, ten to twenty) if that makes sense to your business and will therefore quickly be able to see if this customer has problems that need attention. You just have to make sure you have the right culture at your company so that marking things yellow or red is OK and that your coworkers understand this visual is the fastest way to know when it's time to assign more resources or to bring in management to help fix something before it's too late. Also make sure that salespeople know that bringing in management to help, when needed, is not a reflection of them or their skills as a salesperson.

These dashboards I described above are internal

dashboards. You might review them with your management once a month or quarter with the goal being to find out where there are issues that need to be fixed or if you need to put more resources towards that customer so you can get back on track and do right by your customer. If you are a really forward-thinking company like the company I worked for in Silicon Valley, then you create dashboards that you let your customer fill out before a meeting and then you review the dashboards together. That shows you are collaborative and want to hear their feedback about your products, services, and customer management.

In this scenario, you need to make the dashboard customer-facing and think of the questions that are important to your customers about your company and products or services. Some examples include if you have the right products, if you have the right team in place to support them, if the pricing and margins are fair, if they get the products in a timely manner, or if you have the right type and quantity of inventory in stock for their needs for each season. You can come up with a list of questions and let them pick the red, yellow, or green status on these. Make sure to add some open-ended questions such as, "What could we do to better support you?" "Are there any upcoming company or organizational changes that might affect our relationship?" "What are some upcoming needs that you have that we might be able to help you with?" and "Are there any changes we need to make for you to recommend our product and company?"

If you take this two-way approach, truly want to know

what it is like to do business with you, and are willing to make changes for the better, you will learn things that you didn't know before and can be a better partner to your customers. I promise it will change the relationship from being a one-directional relationship (unidirectional) of you selling them "stuff" to a two-directional relationship (bidirectional) based on feedback and collaboration.

I like to do this by sending the blank dashboard document three to four weeks before an in-person meeting and ask them to complete and return it one week before the meeting. Make sure you give them enough time to be thoughtful and to ask for feedback within their company—and to avoid stressing them out with an unrealistic turnaround. When they have completed the form, start working on your plan and presentation on how you will address their responses.

I like to start with the prior version at the beginning to do a quick recap of what we discussed last time and any changes that have been made to address their concerns. Frame this part as a quick recap so you don't spend the whole time talking about the last meeting, but you do want to remind everyone of what you discussed last time and of any changes (let's hope you did make some changes based on their feedback, or you will not look very customer-focused). Then add the current version of the dashboard to the presentation and spend most of your time on this information during the meeting. If you do meeting agendas (which is a good idea), I suggest the following for a one-hour meeting:

- Introductions (5 mins.)
- Recap of prior dashboard and changes made (10 mins.)
- Discuss current dashboard (40 mins.)
- Review follow-up actions and closing (5 mins.)

This will make a very collaborative face-to-face with management folks from both sides to discuss the health of the relationship and how you can and do constantly improve it. If you are truly customer-focused and willing to change based on feedback, it will show. This is the type of thing that will set you apart from your competition. Just make sure you are committed to listening to feedback (good or bad) and making changes based on their feedback.

As much as dogs hate going to the vet, it's the only way to keep them healthy and fix any health issues before it's too late. It's the same with your customers: checkups, check-ins, and measurements are vital to diagnosing the health of your customer relationships. Be prepared to see what is wrong or offtrack and make changes where needed.

CHAPTER ELEVEN

Dog Park Rules

HOW TO WORK WITH COMPLEX ORGANIZATIONS

ave you ever watched dogs at a dog park navigate
the different personalities of the other dogs and figure out who is going to play with whom and in what
way? Does your dog like to run and roll around with other dogs (like mine)? Is your dog ball-obsessed? Is your
dog a little dog and scared of all of the big-dog energy?
Whatever type of dog you have, dogs at the dog park
have to figure out how to play with different dogs and
navigate complicated relationships. For instance, one of
Oliver's best dog friends, Bruce, is toy-obsessed. Oliver
has learned that if he grabs Bruce's toy, Bruce will happily play tug with him. Oliver doesn't do that with other
dogs—he's more of a rough-and-tumble dog—but that
is how Oliver has learned to play with Bruce. After a few
minutes of tug, they both do other things, but they enjoy
their quick game of tug.

It's the same in sales. Sometimes we have to navigate

a lot of different personalities and we have to learn to "play" differently with different people. In consumer sales, you sell to the end user and often it's a one-time transactional sale, so you are dealing with the evaluator, end user, and the decision-maker all rolled into one. That can be good because you only have to deal with one person. It's simpler than a business-to-business sale where you are often dealing with a large, complex organization and all the people that entails. But that can also be bad because if you haven't done a good job convincing the consumer that yours is the right product for him or her, you don't have anyone else to convince who can weigh in.

If you work in a large organization, you also have to deal with people in different functions within your own company, such as research and development (R&D), marketing, legal, accounting/finance, inventory control, HR, customer service, and so forth. Layer on the management folks in all of those departments and you have to deal with a lot of different people and personalities. This ability to work with different folks is a skill that many sales folks take for granted, but it's not something that most people can do well. I pride myself on this skill and even list it at the top of my resume: "Expert at managing complex, strategic relationships and driving mutually beneficial outcomes."

HOW TO NAVIGATE VARIOUS PERSONALITIES

Like the dogs at the dog park, you may have to "play" with different personalities in different ways to be successful. Not to stereotype, but . . . you may have to be a little more serious and buttoned up with the legal and finance folks than you are with the sales and marketing folks. And you may need to be a little careful about what you say around your HR partners. Although I may be a little more serious with these people, I have certainly had some good belly laughs with some finance, HR, and legal partners.

I also know going into a meeting with the accounting/finance people at either my company or a customer's company, they are going to want to know hard numbers. They will ask about pricing, margins, any discounts we are considering offering, payment terms, our return on investment, and so forth. I make sure to have that information available in case it comes up. Similarly, the legal people from both sides are going to want to talk about contract length, terms, customer requirements, and any deal breakers, so I try to do all of my research before meeting with them so it can be a productive meeting. Know your internal audience and be prepared with the right information to make your case to do what's best for both your company and your customer.

Make sure you treat all of your coworkers as part of your team. Often you feel you are at odds with certain functional groups. (You want the R&D folks to create the products that your customers are asking for, but they have other priorities. You want to close a deal, but your legal team won't agree to a clause in the contract. You just need to sweeten the deal, but the finance folks are standing in your way, and so forth.) Many salespeople treat their cross-functional coworkers as roadblocks to getting a sale, but I flip that theory on its head and make sure I treat them as partners. I try to remember that everyone has their expertise and sometimes it can be at odds with mine as the salesperson. In all of the deals I have negotiated successfully and even some that have gotten the kibosh from the legal or finance teams, I think those folks have always done what is best for the company and I respect them for that. If you treat cross-functional employees in your company like partners and not as roadblocks, you can start to respect them for their expertise (which you probably don't have unless you went to law school or have a finance degree and years of finance expertise), and they will start to respect you for your expertise in return.

Recently, I had a difficult customer who received an invoice for approximately $150 for something she thought would be sent at no charge. Even though it was a small amount, I still went to my finance person to ask her to write it off. When she asked why I wanted her to write it off, I was honest and told her we have had a lot of problems with this customer recently and it would create a lot of goodwill if I could go back and tell them they did not have to pay that invoice.

My finance partner agreed to it because I was honest about the reason, had developed a good relationship with her, and had not asked her to do that type of thing in the past. Had I been adversarial with her in the past or not taken the time and effort to cultivate the relationship and appreciate her expertise, she may have denied my request. I was then able to go back to my customer and tell her I got that invoice written off, and I got a nice, "Thanks, Julie!!!" email back from a customer who was seeing red about our company the day before. So for that small $150 charge that I worked collaboratively with my finance partner to write off, I was able to get a challenging customer relationship back on track.

On a side note, I try to come into each situation or negotiation representing both my customer and my company and strive to create a mutually beneficial outcome. I have to be honest and say I do have financial incentive to see that the deals go through, so I am going to do my best to make that happen, but I won't do any deal that is bad for either my company or the customer. Sometimes the legal and finance folks tell me things I don't want to hear, and you have to understand the culture of your own company well enough to know whether you have to go with their recommendations or if you can factor those recommendations into a larger deal or relationship and override them. If you don't know that answer, ask your boss what the company stance is before overriding either legal or finance.

When I worked in Silicon Valley, we in sales tried our best to follow the legal and finance recommendations, but there were a few times we did not take their advice because other factors were in play that were beyond the legal and finance considerations and were important to consider when making the final decision. I always involved my management team before overriding either legal or finance. We only ended up doing it a couple of times and I stand by those decisions.

Sometimes folks at your own company or at a customer's company are not going to get along. That is just life and you need to learn how to deal with it. You need to figure out the different personalities and which people can't play nice together and deal with it accordingly. Just like the dogs at the dog park, you may need to deal with different people differently.

CHAPTER TWELVE

Bad Dog

HOW TO HANDLE BAD CUSTOMERS

Sometimes it's hard to admit but some dogs, like people, are just bad. Whether it's nature or nurture doesn't really matter. For instance, if your dog bites a child, yours or someone else's, you are probably going to have to figure out a new situation for that dog. Maybe the dog had trauma in their early puppyhood, but in all likelihood you are still going to have to get rid of the dog.

It happens sometimes with customers, too. There are some that, no matter what you do, are never going to be happy with you. If you were at the dog park, you might both bare teeth. Unfortunately, in the business world, baring teeth at your customer would be inappropriate, and bizarre—though sometimes you wish you could. Whether "the customer is always right" philosophy rules at your company might dictate how you handle a bad customer. You also have to take your sales quota into consideration. I have had to bite my tongue so many times in the past when I thought a customer was being unreasonable but I couldn't burn the relationship or I wouldn't have hit my quota. As mentioned in chapter 3, the worst customers are the ones who are not only mean but also realize the power dynamic in sales and exploit it.

As salespeople, we have to put up with more than our fair share of bad customer behavior or those who are just bad apples because we are dependent on our prospects and customers buying from us. I have tried to ignore rude remarks, but if it gets really bad and someone muttered something like, "Idiot," I might say something like, "I'm sorry, it sounded like you called me an idiot, but I don't think that you would do that. Did I mishear you?" That remark either causes them admit to being a jerk or lets them change their story and save face. If they do admit to being a jerk, you have the opportunity to say something like, "Hey, I really want to continue to do business with you, but I do expect some common decency, such as not being called names. Can we agree to reset and start again?" Most people with an iota of empathy will feel like a jerk and try to be a little nicer.

A few times in my career someone has used profanity with me. When that happens, I put my foot down and have—luckily—worked at places where my bosses also found that behavior unacceptable and stood up for me. If it happens, you should escalate it to your boss who, hopefully, will step in to diffuse the situation and let the customer know that using profanity towards someone in your company is unacceptable behavior.

WHAT TO DO IF YOU HAVE A BAD BOSS

There is one thing harder than having a bad customer, and it's having a bad boss. Let me preface this with saying I have had around twenty-five bosses in my career and most were good or great, but a few were not.

Believe it or not, I once had a boss who told me sometimes he gets so mad at me, it's like when you want to kick your dog. "What?" you say? Yes, he really did say that. Who kicks their dog? This was someone who prided himself on being a really good boss. He thought of himself as a real nurturer and mentor who had lots of wisdom and experiences to share with his employees. Sometimes he did teach me things, but what I remember all these years later is that fact that he said he wanted to kick me like a dog (Hello, Michael Vick). Why I didn't run to HR after that, I have no idea, but instead I let him berate me, took his insult without causing a fuss, and felt bad about myself for whatever it was I had done that made him want to kick me.

Early in my career, I had another boss (a man) who insisted that we share a room on a work trip. I was lucky that I had a friend in that city and was able to sleep on the floor in her empty studio apartment (she had just moved in), but it was a much better situation than being in a hotel room with my boss of the opposite sex. As I type this in the post #metoo world, I am appalled that he would suggest that and also appalled that I had almost forgotten about it.

I will say twenty years later that I don't think he was

angling to do anything inappropriate (other than the obvious of asking to share a room) but that it was purely a financial issue. It was a small start-up and he didn't have enough money to pay the bills, so an extra hotel room in a big city was not something he could afford. Ironically, we were on that trip to ask investors for more money, which we got but the company later went belly up. Still, it was a terrible position to put an employee in and just one of many red flags about that start-up.

This same boss asked us to disguise our voices and pretend to be a fictional accounts payable employees when a creditor called to say that the bill in question was about to be paid. I refused but didn't walk out that day. I was in my twenties and it was my first opportunity to be in management and hopefully "make it big" at a start-up, so I put up with more than I should have. My only regret is that I worked there as long as I did with all of those red flags.

In the above-mentioned scenarios, I now realize that those were not isolated situations but part of a trend. I wish I had realized earlier that I needed to get out. I eventually ended up leaving either the role or the company, but I never left fast enough. I also never reported any incidents to HR, which I now realize I should have. All that to say, don't be like me in my twenties. Have the confidence in yourself and your professional abilities to leave and/or report to HR when a boss verbally abuses you, makes you uncomfortable, harasses you, or asks you to do something that would damage your reputation.

If you're currently working under a bad boss, please

promise yourself that you will change your situation as soon as you can. If you can't afford to just walk out, make a plan to get out and focus all of your energy on finding a new job. Go back to chapter 1, "Always Hungry," and read the section on securing a new job. Bad customers are tough, but bad bosses can make your life miserable.

In your career you can't always leave the dog park when a bad dog arrives. However, if you are able to identify the bad dogs and rise above it or set boundaries when necessary, you can continue to be a positive and productive salesperson and not get dragged into the mud by a bad dog.

CHAPTER THIRTEEN

Stay Hydrated

FOCUS ON WORK/LIFE BALANCE

As every dog knows, after you play hard at the dog park, you need to hydrate yourself. When he gets thirsty, my dog Oliver slurps up the water in the travel water bowl I bring and sometimes even puts his face in it to get his nose wet. You can't help but laugh because it's a funny—but very effective—way to cool off. He knows when to take a water break, and once he's re-hydrated, he's ready to get back out there and play with his dog friends again. It's the same with humans. After we've worked hard, we need to take the time to enjoy the "life" part of work/life balance.

As a wife and mother, I have to be intentional about making sure that I have a good work/life balance and not to work too much. In sales, your job never really stops and you could work twenty-four hours a day. How-ever, according to the law of diminishing returns, if you worked twenty-four hours a day, you would not be three times as productive as those who work eight hours a day. At the same time, someone who works twelve hours a day might be twice as effective as someone who works eight hours a day. Then there is that person who can do more in four hours than others do in ten. To a certain extent, output depends on the person more than the hours worked, but we all have to find the balance between what we feel we need to accomplish, what we can accomplish in a day, and our long-term health and happiness.

I give a lot to my sales job, but sometimes I have to step back and make sure I prioritize my life outside work in order to maintain a healthy balance. We all have different situations, but here is what I do. I try to give my attention to my job approximately eight or nine hours a day, but because I have a traveling sales job, some days I work twelve to fourteen hours and then other days I might be so exhausted from traveling that I only work seven hours. I try to look at it holistically. I might work sixty-plus hours some weeks with lots of travel, but then I might try to slow down the next week, and get my energy back, and put more time towards my family.

TAKE CARE OF YOURSELF OR YOU'LL NEVER SURVIVE LONG TERM IN SALES

As you focus on the "life" part on the work/life balance, find out what sustains you and do more of that. For instance, I love volunteering in my children's classrooms. Because my work schedule is unpredictable, I can't commit to the same time slot every week, but I can keep my eyes out for volunteer opportunities that work with my schedule. I also know my twelve-year-old doesn't want me to volunteer in his class any more, but my nine-year-old loves it when I volunteer in her PE class or on field trips, and my seven-year-old is happy to see me at any time. My spouse also enjoys volunteering at our children's schools, and she and I have found a method of splitting volunteer opportunities that works for us. She has her own business and is usually able to work from home, so we look at our schedules for the upcoming week and see if one of us can volunteer in the classroom. I sometimes go weeks without getting in the classroom, but when I do get in and volunteer, it fills my bucket and makes me happy. I also get to know my kids' teachers and their friends, which is invaluable as a parent. Lastly, I get a boost from seeing firsthand how my sales job in education benefits kids.

I have realized two things in my career. First, I hope to enjoy my job but don't want to be defined or remembered only by it, and second, I can be uber-productive when I want to be. I want to be remembered by who I am, what I gave back to my family, friends, and society, and for having (hopefully) left the world a better place than how I found it. To me, the most important thing in my life is family. Following that is friends and other relationships. I always felt blessed for having been born into a big family. I'm the youngest of five; my dad was one of seven; my mom was one of six; and I have twenty-nine first cousins. Growing up, my parents always valued and emphasized family. Since I had so many playmates to choose from, if I didn't want to play with one kid; there were always plenty more to play with. Now that I am married and have my own kids, I try to follow my parents' lead and emphasize the importance of family. My kids think their grandparents are the best, their aunts and uncles are all so cool, and spending time with their cousins is like finding gold.

In my life, I have also learned that I can be uber-productive if I want to be. I would like to say that my energy and focus is at 100 percent every work day, but that's not true. Sometimes I'm only at 50 percent and sometimes I'm at what feels like 200 percent. Below I give some tips for increasing your productivity. One thing I have learned about myself is that I can get depleted from doing sales and traveling day in and day out. I sometimes have to slow down and not schedule so many meetings outside of the house or take a break from work to walk my dog, get the much-needed haircut, or run a household errand. If I do take a break, I can kick into hyper-focused mode and make up for lost time. As mentioned earlier, those who work the longest are not always the most productive and, sometimes, they're the least productive.

One way I increase my productivity is to schedule an "anchor" meeting and then schedule "cluster" meetings. Here is how this works. I plan to visit one of my customers and schedule a meeting with one person there. Then I reach out to two to five other people and say I have a meeting there on a certain day and am hoping I can stop by and say hi and see if they need anything from me. Since I have taken the pressure off by saying that I will already be on-site, they are more likely to meet with me.

I often get three to five meetings that day at one location where I originally just had one meeting. One thing I have found in sales, if you can get in front of the customer, you will always learn at least one thing—and maybe you will make a sale.

Make sure you remember that it's not the ones who work the longest but those who are the most focused and efficient who get the most done. I remember when I worked in Silicon Valley and there was this twenty-something guy who was always the last one at work (sometimes by hours). I think he liked the badge of being the "hardest worker." After working with him for a while, I realized he wasn't the hardest worker at all. He was extremely social and spent a lot of time talking to colleagues, so he needed to stay as late as he did to get his work done. Where the rest of us could work eight to ten hours and get things done, he had to work ten to twelve hours to get the same amount done.

So if you are burned out and need to knock off work a little early, spend time with your family and friends, or run out and get that much-needed haircut, do it. Just make sure you are a little more efficient the next day to make up for it. Use my anchor and cluster meeting technique if it's appropriate to your business and you'll be more productive by getting in front of more people than you would have if you had just gone out for one meeting. Also, stay focused and on task when you are working. As you are thinking about work/life balance, remember that you need to put your safety mask on first before you can help others.

Another way to nourish yourself is by spending time on your creative pursuits or hobbies. Being a salesperson was never my career goal and didn't align with any of my hobbies, but it was a path I found myself on after college. For the most part, it has been good to me. I've always liked to travel and meet new people, and those have been two things that I have been able to do throughout my sales career. (Although now that I have kids, the traveling part is less fun and more of a nuisance than anything else.) However, I also have a lot of untapped creative energy, so I am trying some new ventures on the side (such as writing this book) that allow me to explore my more creative side without quitting my day job. I started putting two to three hours aside a week at night or on weekends to devote to things I'm passionate about.

I have started blogging at my two websites, www.the ordinarymom.com and www.thesidehustlejourney.com. On www.theordinarymom.com, I blog about my life as a parent, which allows me to write, think about how to be a better parent, and help other people—all things that are important to me. On www.thesidehustlejourney. com, I blog about ways that I—and others—can earn extra income. Discovering that I had other passions I wanted to pursue outside of my day job has given me more energy as opposed to taking it away, even though I have put more on my plate. I feel good knowing I'm spending what precious little extra time I have on things that bring me joy and give me energy.

This is just one way I've found to focus on my work/ life balance in the last two years, and I am so thrilled I have. As Nike says, "Just do it," and I did and I'm happy I did. Make sure you figure out a work/life balance that works for you and you discover your passions so that you don't end up with "She was a hard worker" or "She loved to work" on your gravestone.

In the same vein, I don't pressure my kids to think of what they want to be when they grow up. I want them to do what they love and, ideally, find a career that aligns with their passions. I know that's not always possible, but I want my kids to dream big and see if they can turn their dreams into a career. My seven-year-old loves food and has started to cook, so she is hoping to be a chef. My nine-year-old is an athlete and she wants to be an American Ninja Warrior. My twelve-year-old loves movies and wants to be a filmmaker. My twelve-year-old said the other day, "I might have to get another job as I'm trying to break into the film industry, so I may want to be a masseuse, too." To all of these aspirations, we say, "That's awesome. I hope you find something you love that you can turn into your career."

You need to be like the dogs at the dog park and stick your nose in the water when you're thirsty. Do whatever you need to do to stay hydrated and keep a good work/life balance.

Shake Off the Mud

CHANGE YOUR MINDSET

I have watched my dog get knocked down at the dog park more times than I can count. He always gets right back up and jumps right back into the thick of things. If he gets dirt or mud on him, he shakes it off and gets back to playing. When you get knocked down in sales, picking yourself up, dusting yourself off, and getting back in the ring is one of the most important things you can do. Dogs know that instinctively, but humans often get bogged down in why they got knocked down, who knocked them down, what could they have done differently, wondering if anyone saw them get knocked down, thinking maybe it's better to just stay down, hoping no one sees the mud on their pants, and so forth.

We think too much about all the reasons why we got knocked down and whose fault it was (certainly not our own), but we often don't just get back up and get back in the ring. Since sales jobs are tough, getting knocked down a lot is part of the job. Maybe we should start including it in the sales job description: "Boxing experience a plus." Therefore, you need to be resilient and develop thick skin. As mentioned in previous chapters, sales jobs are also innately customer focused and sometimes we have to deal with challenging people.

If you stay down, your sales career will be short-lived. These knocks can be small (e.g., someone saying no to purchasing your product after you have spent a lot of time and effort showing them the benefits), medium (e.g., you just can't seem to get this particular customer to buy anything you offer, even when you have been working with them and cultivating the relationship for years), or big (e.g., a customer leaves a voicemail for your boss's boss saying they think you are terrible and they want you transferred off the account). All of these examples have happened to me in the last two weeks! Yes, I'm serious.

I had a one-two-three punch and was barely hanging onto the ring. I was almost ready to throw in the towel with a "woe is me, this is too hard" attitude. But I have enough experience and, hopefully, maturity to step back and remember that my job is to sell educational curriculum to school districts and that schools had recently gone back in session. Tensions are high when the administrators and teachers get back to school and their curriculum is not there or not what they expected it to be.

Had I been new to this job or not familiar with the cycle of the education industry, I might have quit. But this ain't my first rodeo (as my dad would say), and I know that as much prep as I do in the summer to get ready for back-to-school craziness, there are always going to be issues during this season. What I try to remember is that out of my fifty or so customers, one might hate me, nine might be angry at my company and take it out on me, but forty are very happy with me and the value that I provide them.

And as for the customer who refuses to work with me, I have been around enough to know that it could be a blessing in disguise if they get assigned to another salesperson. They are a low-revenue contract that takes up a lot of my time, and a couple of people who work there are pretty mean-spirited. When I am calm and can think about this at a higher level, I know I need to say "good riddance" and spend my time and energy on customers who I can help teach children successfully and grow the business. That's easier said than done, but I don't want one bad apple to drain me of energy or make me feel that I'm not a good salesperson.

For this particular customer, I asked my boss if he'd consider giving them to an inside sales rep. Inside sales reps are my associates who do not travel like I do and sit in the office most days helping customers. I think that is exactly what this customer wants: someone who will answer the phone every time they call, which I'm not able to do as I am often traveling or in customer meetings or trainings. It's hard when a customer complains to your management about you, but sometimes it's a blessing in disguise if your management stands up for you and realizes the relationship may not be the best fit for either you or your customer.

BE PREPARED TO ZIG INSTEAD OF ZAG

At times in my career, I have gotten to the point at a job where I just did not think I could go in the next day and do the same thing again. It wasn't that I had a bad boss or product to sell—I was just bored or frustrated at times. I remember being in my twenties and thinking if I went to work that day and was not happy, I might have to quit and find another job. At the time, I lived in a ski town in the Rockies and was lucky enough to have worked at several local software companies during the eight years I lived there. I had no family to support, low house pay-ments, and an old car that was paid off, so I probably could have quit just because I felt like it. The problem was I wasn't in a place where I could find an equal or better job easily.

For example when I later lived in Silicon Valley, I could literally walk next door and get an equal or better job. To that point, Google actually started in a small of-fice next door to my company and if I would have gone next door to work there back then, I might be on the beach in the Caribbean drinking mai tais right now. Or maybe it wouldn't have been a good fit and I would have left before becoming a Googleaire, but I can still dream.

Instead, I stayed at that job in the Rockies for six years and the job in Silicon Valley for fifteen years, so I never did walk next door to find a new job, and I have yet to quit on a whim. The reason I stayed at both jobs even though I was sometimes frustrated with my customers or my company was that I instinctively knew I needed to be careful thinking the grass is always greener some-where else. I worked both jobs with some really amazing people and knew I'd be going to an unknown (to me) company and people. Though both jobs were custom-er-facing, I can't remember the names of many of my customers from those years (company names, yes, but customer names, not so much). But I remember the folks I worked with and for and most of them were amazing. I learned a lot from them and laughed a lot with them, which I find equally important. Now, if you're truly in a bad situation, make a plan and leave, as I've said in other chapters. But if you're just bored or frustrated, see if you can change your mindset without leaving your company, especially if you don't have a better position lined up. As a side note, during my time at the Silicon Valley job, I got married and had kids and, let me tell you, it's a lot harder to walk away from a good job when you have a family to think about.

Another way to exercise flexible thinking is to change how you look at a problem to see if you can propose a new solution. I was in a situation recently with one of my large accounts that could have been a nightmare, but I changed the way I looked at the problem, thought stra-tegically, and turned it around to create a positive out-come. A school district was looking at our product and doing a "pilot." For a pilot, we send a school or district a subset of our materials for free, and they test it with a small number of teachers and students to see if it will work for them. This customer was piloting a new science product. For science, teachers want to do hands-on labs, so we created some lab kits for them to test. The customer wanted to test some labs that we had not yet created kits for, as the product was still being created. I had originally told the customer that we would custom build the kits for them.

Long story short is that I started down the path of creating the custom kits with the help of some work associates, and it was overwhelming. It was causing me more stress than anything else at my job at that point. I stepped back and realized I had to go back to the customer and propose another solution. I told my customer that I had underestimated what it would take to custom build the kits, and by the time we got them done, the pilot might have ended, which would not benefit the teachers. I asked if she would ask her pilot teachers if they could evaluate the product on the kits they already had (each teacher had received one pre-built kit) or if it would help to have more of the pre-built kits. I told her I didn't want to do anything that would negatively affect the outcome of the purchase decision, but I needed to figure out a different solution than what I had originally proposed. I didn't know how she would react, but she talked to her teachers and some were fine with what they already had while some wanted more of the pre-built kits, which I could easily order. In the midst of feeling completely overwhelmed, I was luckily able to step back, think strategically to come up with a new solution, and save a lot of stress for myself and money for my company without jeopardizing the outcome of the sale.

If your fur gets a little dirty, instead of making a big

stink, try to shake off the mud and get back into it. If another dog judges you because you have a little mud on you, that may not be a dog you want to play with anyway. And if things don't go as planned, stay flexible and consider changing your mindset. Zig instead of zag, but keep your eyes on the prize and eventually you will reach it.

CHAPTER FIFTEEN

Sometimes Their Bark Is Worse Than Their Bite

DEALING WITH ANGRY CUSTOMERS

You know how a dog at the dog park who looks aggressive and greets other dogs with a fierce bark can turn out to be a real softy? Some dogs and people, whether because of anxiety, low self-esteem, stress, cultural upbringing, or what have you, jump into situations aggressively to show their dominance. It can be scary to deal with an aggressive dog or person, but often we just have to step back to let them vent and see if we can connect with them to calm them down. We are not talking about serially bad or mean-spirited customers here, as in chapter 12, "Bad Dog," but customers who are situationally upset and relationships you can salvage.

Unfortunately, part of sales is dealing with angry or difficult customers. I have found that most of my difficult customers are usually only situationally difficult. They are not always difficult people, but something (or many things) may have happened to push them over the edge. When I look back at whom I've considered difficult customers in the hardware/software world (where I've spent most of my career), it was really because they were people who had not received what they wanted when they wanted it or did not feel they were heard.

If you have a difficult customer, see if you notice a pattern. Like many yellers, maybe they just want to be heard. Maybe they were the bully at the playground because it was the only way to get attention. Or maybe they were bullied and have taken on a bully's persona, or no one in their family listened to them when they were kids. Whatever the reason is, if you can look for patterns and either change the situation before you know it's about to turn bad or try to be empathetic about whatever's bothering them, you might be able to turn a difficult customer into an ally. They are used to people pulling away or avoiding them, so if you are able to predict and defuse their bad behavior or make a connection, they might not be so difficult with you and you might find they want to do business with you.

I find that usually prospects and customers are not difficult up front. As I mentioned in previous chapters, customers can become difficult post-sale when something did not work out the way they had assumed or had been told it would. One way to head off a customer becoming difficult is to set very clear expectations. If they want to order your product but need it tomorrow (or next week) and you know that's not possible, do not make the sale until you set the correct expectations that they will not be able to get the product by their deadline.

I promise you that it's not worth getting the sale if you know you can't hit the customer's deadline. You are going to have to do some probing, as described in chapter 4. You might say, "I know you said you need it by next Monday, but can you help me understand why that date is the deadline and what would happen if it didn't arrive by then?" Often you will find out that many deadlines are self-imposed by the customer and aren't hard deadlines. They may have created a timeline for the purchase and implementation that was just a date someone put on a spreadsheet, so there may be some wiggle room. Or the customer wants it next week because they are going on vacation the following week and they want to make sure it's been delivered by the time they return—you can probably work through this one. Or it's a birthday gift and needs to arrive by someone's birthday and the timing really is a deal breaker—you probably can't work through this one. By probing to see if their deadline is a real deadline, you might be able to work with the customer to reset expectations, or you may realize that you cannot hit their deadline and need to tell them up front and directly that they may need to purchase elsewhere.

If that probing didn't happen, the order wasn't placed in a timely manner, shipping was delayed, or there was some other reason that things didn't go as smoothly as hoped, you might have an angry customer on your hands. As their salesperson, you are most likely the single point of contact or at least the main contact at your company, so you are going to get the brunt of the anger even if these mistakes were not your fault.

Unfortunately, these situations happen all the time in all companies. The customer did not start off difficult but became difficult because of something that happened. In these scenarios, I try my best to allow the customer to vent, not take it personally, and not say that it was someone else's fault. Most of the time, they are just upset because things didn't go the way that they expected, and they need to go through the process of being upset (and possibly mourning a kind of loss) before moving on.

I recently had a customer who was a teacher who was upset that the product the district ordered was not exactly what he had tried out (or piloted, as we call it) the year before. He didn't feel like he was being heard, and he complained all the way up to the superintendent of the school district. I had never had a teacher escalate a complaint up to the superintendent, so I got my boss involved to help me defuse the situation. The superintendent let my boss know that this teacher is not good with change and the fact that we changed something really threw him off. My boss has a daughter with autism who also finds change difficult, so he immediately understood that we needed to approach the teacher and the situation differently. Even though we thought the new version was better than what the teacher had tried the year before, we gave him the option to go back to the older version. He said that he did not want to make the change to the new version, so we were able to figure it out as a team and get him a version that was just like what he piloted and, eventually, all was well. It helped me to hear that the teacher wasn't trying to be difficult but that we had thrown him off by not giving him the exact thing he thought he was going to get. That knowledge allowed me to change my mindset from being irritated that he went to the big wig in the district to having empathy for him and approaching him in a more connected way.

In hindsight, I was also glad I looped in my boss as he immediately understood the situation since change is hard for his daughter as well. Later, he was also able to clear some internal roadblocks to allow us to change the product much more quickly than I could have. I was also glad that I was able to pivot to being able to understand the customer's point of view and get him a product that worked for him.

IT'S NOT YOU

Sometimes customers are difficult not because of their personalities but because you just can't crack their account. I have an account that we never win their business. We go in time and time again, they evaluate our products, and they always go with someone else. I decided early on that I would not let them deter me, and through good products, hard work, and professionalism, I would one day win their business and trust. Every time I get turned down by them, I have picked myself up, dusted myself off, and gone back in the next time optimistic that this is the time (isn't that a definition of insanity?). I have put my best foot forward and always make sure I'm super responsive and professional with the ten or so contacts I have there. Though I've built up three years of "nos" from them, I have slowly and steadily built up their trust and currently have four deals I'm working on with them. I always have an anchor meeting and then try to have cluster meetings whenever I go on site, which has been about once a week lately (which is a lot). I was there recently to train them on a product I'm hoping they will buy, and three times someone popped into the room and asked if I had a second to meet. The head person at the account was in the training and said to the teachers being trained, "Sorry for the interruptions, but word is out that Julie is here and everyone wants a word with her." It felt amazing. I had finally gotten to the point where they heard I was on site and wanted to see me. Fingers crossed that I win their business, and if I do, I will have truly turned around what we had deemed a difficult customer account.

In so many cases, it's not you as the salesperson that is the problem. It's not even the customer. It's just the situation or the timing. Sometimes, the customer just needs to vent and being a sounding board is part of being a salesperson. I think of how sometimes I just need to allow myself to feel angry and share my frustrations with someone, and then I can move on. Sometimes I will even say to a friend or family member, "Can you just give me a few minutes to vent about something that happened at work and just insert a few supportive phrases, so I can get this out and move on?"

It really works most of the time. You should try it. You can also vent to your dog, but please be careful that you do not sound angry or they will think you are angry with them. But venting in a calm voice while petting your dog and scratching him or her behind the ears can be very therapeutic to both of you. Just another reason that dogs are amazing.

Be True to Yourself: Don't Try to Be a Pitbull If You Are a Poodle

HOW TO NAVIGATE THE OLD BOYS NETWORK
IF YOU AREN'T PART OF IT

'll just say it: sales is an old boys network in most industries, especially at the higher levels. I have been in sales my whole career and have had to deal with the fact that most of the time I'm an outsider because I'm female. When I was working in Silicon Valley, they didn't know how to pay me when I was out on maternity leave because, as my boss said, "We're not used to having female salespeople at your level." Wow.

Working in sales in Silicon Valley for nearly fifteen years was eye-opening. It made me realize that many people I worked with in sales were white men, married with kids, whose wives either did not work or their jobs took a back seat to their husbands' job. This meant a lot of things but one thing I noticed in particular was that some of the men I worked with in sales had little household responsibilities when they got home from work, which felt very 1950s to me. They knew that when they got home (whatever time it was) dinner would be on the table, the kids would have been dropped off and picked up from daycare or school, their drycleaning would have been picked up so they'd have something to wear the next day, and the house would be clean. It just all magically happened behind the scenes.

Now compare that to the scenario that most working moms face: wake up early to make lunches and get your kids ready for daycare or school, drive your kids there, get to work at a decent hour, and look like you are calm, cool, and collected even though you might have peanut butter and jelly (or vomit) on your shirt. Then work all day and try to stay focused on your job and not on the fact that your daughter had an upset stomach and the school might call you to pick her up or you need to do errands on your lunch break because you don't have anything to make for dinner that night. Make sure you leave work at a certain time every day to pick up your kids from daycare or school so you don't get charged for every minute you are late (or from after-school care or a babysitter because who can get them by the time school gets out at 2:30 or 3:00 p.m.?). Make dinner, get the kids to do their homework, get ready for whatever project or special food is needed for the next school day, get the kids ready for bed and then to sleep, clean the kitchen, throw in some laundry, and, in a perfect world, straighten up the house. And you probably didn't have time to walk the dog (again).

You will be lucky to maybe find a few minutes of

solitude to read, check social media or watch Netflix before going to sleep and starting the whole thing over again the next day. On top of that, many sales jobs require extensive travel, which is why you don't see as many women (or at least women of childbearing age) in them because who's going to pick up the slack at home when they are traveling? The partners or spouses, you say? Not in most relationships.

I'd like to think that what I just said is a gross misinterpretation of what is happening in the U.S. today, but I challenged myself to think of families where both parents work, it was the first marriage for both, they have young kids (i.e. under ten), and they split household and childcare responsibilities 50/50. I can think of only a handful of families who do and that's out of hundreds of families I know. I hope I'm wrong and really lots of families are splitting all the responsibilities at home and with the kids and just not making a big deal of it.

Indeed, my in-laws were splitting childcare and family responsibilities over forty years ago. My mother-in-law had a big corporate law job and my father-in-law (whom I never met because he passed away before I met my wife) was in academia and had more flexibility, so he did more around the house and with the kids. I grew up in a traditional house where my dad worked outside the home and my mom worked by rearing the kids and doing everything else to make the household run smoothly (unpaid, of course).

I am always surprised that even though so many families today have two working adults, the woman is still expected to do most of the child-related responsibilities and housework. My wife and I might have an advantage because gender doesn't enter into the equation. We both work and we try to divvy up the childcare and household responsibilities evenly. Some years I do more at home and some years she does more, and we adjust based on who has the more demanding job at the time. I will say that now that I am in sales in the educational publishing business I work with more women than men and the women are doing extensive travel, although only a few have young kids

Navigating the old boys network can be a challenge if you're not part of it. I tend to downplay what I have going on outside of work because I don't want to be seen as unfocused or not as dedicated as my male peers. It makes me mad sometimes that I have felt like I've had to downplay my home life (and it makes my wife really mad, like seeing-red mad), but it's what I feel like I have had to do, especially when I was working in sales in Silicon Valley with mostly male counterparts. Don't get me wrong, I worked with some of the best and most kind men of my career during that time and a lot of them are still friends.

I am now in educational sales and I work with a lot more women than men but both the men and women, many of who are former teachers, are more open about talking about their kids and/or childcare issues at work. I have learned who is truly interested in hearing updates on my life and kids and who is not and I share accordingly. In this industry, it seems talking or not talking about family at work is not along gender lines, which I like so I get to hear different stories from both men and women about how they are balancing (or not balancing) their work and home lives.

Different industries are different about talking about work/life balance. I remember when we had our first child and I went out on maternity leave. As I mentioned, I was working in high tech in Silicon Valley at the time. I thought I'd send a note to my customers that I'd had a baby and decided to attach a picture of my newborn to make it a little more personal. I got a few "congratulations" but also got one, "Please don't send me any more personal emails" from one of my male customers.

Compare that to my wife who was in the healthcare industry and worked mainly with women at the time. When she sent a similar note, she got comments like, "Congratulations, your baby is gorgeous," "You now will always be a parent above anything else," and "Your life has changed and will never be the same. Enjoy the ride." We laughed at the time, but it was a little sad that I wanted to share the biggest news in my life with my customers and got mostly no response and even one nasty reply. We have a long way to go to make parenting more respected in the workplace, and I know that part of that is speaking up about what it means to be a working parent, but it's hard to implement change and mostly I'm just too tired to take a stand.

Know yourself and remember to be true to yourself at the office and with your customers. Don't try to be a pitbull if you are a poodle. Because once the fake poodle fur gets blown off on a windy day, the other dogs will figure it out anyway. Be your authentic self and the other dogs will love you for who you are.

CHAPTER SEVENTEEN

Don't Forget to Roll Around in the Mud, Get Dirty, and Have Some Fun

WORK HARD BUT DON'T FORGET TO STOP AND LAUGH

Dogs know how to have fun. They are not worried about messing up their fur or getting a little mud on them. They just want to have fun and play with other dogs. That is something that humans, mainly adults, forget to do. It's no different with sales. We are usually so focused on selling our products, hitting our quotas, and doing right by our customers that we often forget to enjoy the ride. The most memorable times of my career have been the times I laughed with customers or associates and made true connections.

If you are really lucky, you are able to laugh so hard it becomes a belly laugh. Just today a customer told me in a sassy voice that I should get back to our customer service department and tell them off for sending me an incorrect quote for her. She said if I wouldn't do it, she would. It made me laugh in a situation that could have been painful (we had sent her the wrong quote, after all, and money tends to make people serious), but the customer has been very happy with the extra effort I've put forth with them recently and she was prepared to fight my internal battle for me. The way we came together in a potential stressful situation to jointly figure out a solution defused the stress, and the customer actually inserted some humor, which doesn't happen often.

IT'S OK TO SHARE CUSTOMER STORIES, BUT BE APPROPRIATE AND NEVER MEAN

Although I only sometimes laugh with customers, I spend a lot of time laughing with my associates. In sales there are always stories (frankly many salespeople get into sales because they like to tell stories, myself included). Just last month, I was commiserating with an associate about how stressful this time of year is in my job, and I told her how a customer left a voicemail for my boss's boss complaining about me. "That's nothing," she said. "Last week a customer emailed the CEO complaining about me." Our division of the company had just sold, and so we are no longer under the parent company (or that CEO), so we started laughing hysterically about how the customer complained to the wrong CEO. It's like complaining to the Coke CEO about something someone at Pepsi did. Who cares?

You do need to know where to draw the line, though. Make sure you are laughing at situations or something funny a customer may have said or did. Don't go down the rabbit hole of making fun of your customers. It's a lot like gossip. It may seem fun at the time to partake in with others, but you always look back and regret your lapse in judgement.

I tend to be self-deprecating, so before I close, I want to say that I'm not a terrible salesperson. I've only had three customers complain to management about me in thirty years, so I think that's a pretty good track record. Before last month, it was only two in thirty years. I work hard and try to be the best salesperson I can be for my customers, but I need to let off some steam occasionally because my job, like most sales jobs, can be stressful. I find that sharing horror stories with associates and realizing that we all have similar stories is a healthy thing to do. And I always love a good belly laugh. My laugh lines around my eyes confirm that.

I went to college at a small liberal arts school on the East Coast, which I'll call X College to make this point. While I was there the college president was an amazing British woman with a crisp English accent. Her favorite saying was, "At X College, we work hard and we play hard." Imagine that being said in a beautiful British accent with every word enuciated. It really resonated with me. That motto has stayed with me throughout my life and career, and I hear her voice saying it in my head often as a reminder to work hard but play hard, too. And to me, playing hard also includes laughing.

Make sure you make time and room in your sales job to roll around in the mud, get your fur dirty, and have some fun. Dogs have figured out that connecting with others and having fun are the keys to happiness. We should all remember that life is short, and we need to enjoy the journey with the people, and dogs, that we love.

About the Author

JULIE HICKEY, MBA, is a mom, wife, daughter, sister, friend, dog owner, career salesperson, book lover, traveler, entrepreneur, writer and blogger on www.theordinarymom.com and www. thesidehustlejourney.com. She lives in Northern California with her wife, 3 kids, and her dog, Oliver.

photo: Nicole Wickens at Green Door Photography
www.greendoorphotography.com

CPSIA information can be obtained
at www.ICGtesting.com
Printed in the USA
LVHW091536040521
686462LV00017B/240